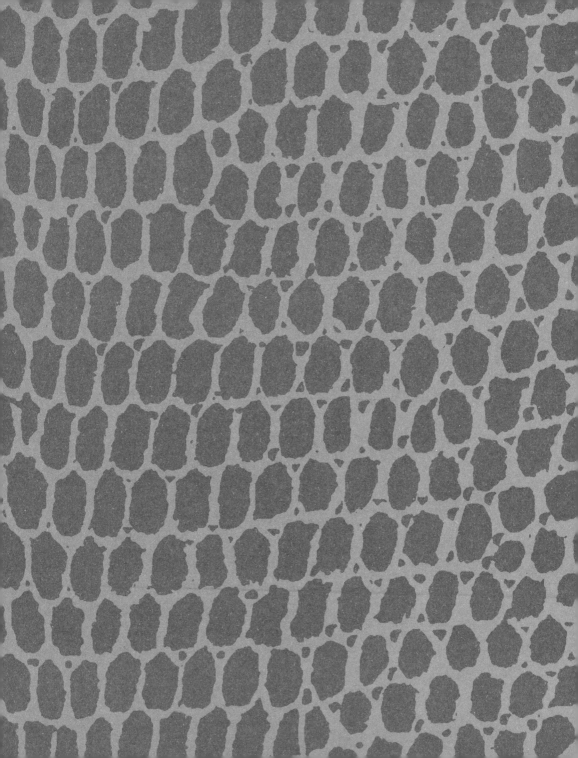

Animal Planet®

Aquarium
Care of
Cichlids

CLAUDIA DICKINSON

Aquarium Care of Cichlids

Project Team
Editors: Ryan Greene, David E. Boruchowitz
Copy Editor: Neale Pronek
Design concept: Leah Lococo Ltd., Stephanie Krautheim
Design layout: Angela Stanford
Chapter 7 written by David E. Boruchowitz

T.F.H. Publications
President/CEO: Glen S. Axelrod
Executive Vice President: Mark E. Johnson
Publisher: Christopher T. Reggio
Production Manager: Kathy Bontz

T.F.H. Publications, Inc.
One TFH Plaza
Third and Union Avenues
Neptune City, NJ 07753

Discovery Communications, Inc.
    Book Development Team
Maureen Smith, Executive Vice President & General
    Manager, Animal Planet
Carol LeBlanc, Vice President, Licensing
Elizabeth Bakacs, Vice President, Creative Services
Peggy Ang, Vice President, Animal Planet Marketing
Caitlin Erb, Licensing Specialist

Printed and bound in China.
07 08 09 10 11 1 3 5 7 9 8 6 4 2
Library of Congress Cataloging-in-Publication Data
Dickinson, Claudia.
Cichlids / Claudia Dickinson.
      p. cm. – (Animal Planet pet care library)
  Includes index.
  ISBN 978-0-7938-3777-9 (alk. paper)
  1. Cichlids. I. Title.
  SF458.C5D53 2007
  639.3'774–dc22
2006100757

This book has been published with the intent to provide accurate and authoritative information in regard to the
subject matter within. While every reasonable precaution has been taken in preparation of this book, the author
and publisher expressly disclaim responsibility for any errors, omissions, or adverse effects arising from the use or
application of the information contained herein. The techniques and suggestions are used at the reader's discretion and are not to be considered a substitute for veterinary care. If you suspect a medical problem consult your
veterinarian.

The Leader In Responsible Animal Care For Over 50 Years!™
www.tfh.com

Table of Contents

Introduction

Welcome to the fascinating world of cichlids (pronounced "sik-lids"), the most diverse, interesting, and intriguing of all fishes! You are about to embark on a remarkable journey from which you will never look back. By researching your subject before you begin, you are taking the first step toward success with your cichlids.

This book will teach you the basic ins and outs of keeping cichlids—but don't stop there. The Resources section at the end offers a list of informative web sites, organizations, and other books to help you on your way. There are also local and national clubs you can join to share the camaraderie, experience, and knowledge of other hobbyists.

Cichlids have a reputation for being ruffians, but once you understand the basic needs of these fishes through an awareness of their natural instincts and way of life in their wild habitats, you will realize why cichlids act as they do within our aquariums. If reading this book sets you on the road to success with your first cichlid aquarium, these pages will have served their purpose well and can be referred back to in the years ahead. Once you are on that proper path, the captivating world of cichlids is certain to bring you a lifetime of enjoyment that is filled with the richest of rewards.

But be careful! If left unchecked, one day the cichlid addiction may overtake you, too, and before you know it you will find that you have turned into a true cichlidophile!

Chapter 1

Why Cichlids?

Countless hobbyists in the United States and across the globe are captivated by the allure of cichlids. The attraction is so great that it compels cichlidophiles to travel hundreds, even thousands, of miles to gather together at national conventions, enjoying the camaraderie and forming a common bond over all things cichlid. But just exactly what defines these fishes, causing them to reign so supremely over all others? Once you have kept these marvelous creatures in your own tanks, you will most certainly understand what the craze is all about, for cichlids offer a diversity of colors, sizes, shapes, and personalities like no other fishes.

A Bit of History

The year was 1895, and the aquarium hobby was thriving with the passion and fervor of expectancy and new discovery. Novel fishes were arriving on the scene at a frenetic pace and being distributed across the country by rail. Reports in America's foremost aquarium magazine at that time relayed spawning narratives of the "Brazilian zebra fish"—or "chanchito," as it would come to be known—in Germany one year earlier, as well as news of this cichlid's having been imported into and bred in the United States.

A hardy and adaptable fish, the chanchito was able to weather the experimental stages of our hobby because it endured well the rigors of cold water, low oxygen, and high levels of dissolved waste. Not all cichlids would have fared so well in this environment, which was poorly regulated in those innocent, ill-informed times, but it exemplifies the forgiving nature of some species of cichlids.

As the twentieth century rolled around, the art of aquarium keeping in general was just coming into its heyday. More and more fishes were being discovered overseas even as techniques of successfully transporting them continued to improve. Enthusiasm soared as myriads of cichlid species from South and Central America and West Africa—and new information on how to care

Old News

The chanchito was the first cichlid to be introduced into the aquarium hobby, and only the second tropical fish ever to be kept in home aquaria. The paradisefish was the first.

for them—became available, and the domesticated cichlid flourished.

Surviving into the post-World War II era, the aquarium hobby rebounded with more vitality than ever in the 1950s and 60s. The brilliantly colored cichlids from the Rift Lakes of Africa were all the rage, with new imports from Lake Malawi and Lake Tanganyika being discovered at every turn of the head. In 1968 the tremendous passion for these fishes brought together a group of dedicated cichlidophiles who formed the

Keeping cichlids exploded in popularity in the 1950s and has been riding high ever since.

American Cichlid Association, which remains today's leader in international cichlid organizations.

New World cichlids—those that come from the Americas, as opposed to the African and Asian, or Old World, cichlids—began a comeback in the late 80s and 90s, as aquarists who had been attracted to the hobby through African Rift Lake cichlids began to look for something new and those who had kept New World cichlids originally were ready to return to these old favorites or try the more recent discoveries. Today you will find a fairly even spread of interest among hobbyists for cichlids from all regions.

Cichlids are Smart!

Cichlids are, beyond a doubt, smarter than any other species of freshwater fishes, and this is a huge part of why they are the most popular and entertaining as well. Quickly learning to recognize you, your cichlids will race to the front of the tank in an exuberant greeting when you walk into the room. Of course, it helps that more often than not your appearance means that a tasty morsel will be dropped into the tank. Cichlid intelligence goes far beyond the association with food, though, as a single cichlid, housed with no other fish in the tank, will form a special bond with its keeper that rivals that of a pet dog or cat.

Some of the larger South American cichlids have even been known to enjoy having their sides stroked by their keepers, and many cichlids will come up to nibble and play with a quiet hand

Cichlid Lovers Assemble!

You will find information on how you can become a part of that celebrated cadre of cichlidophiles, the American Cichlid Association, in the Resources section in the back of this book.

that is placed gently on the substrate of their tank. However, beware if there are fry in the tank, as that same hand is likely to be attacked with ferocious aggression in defense of the young.

Sitting in a chair in front of your cichlid tank will bring you as many hours of enjoyment as watching television or going out to the movies might bring to some. Just make a cold drink or a hot cup of tea and sit back and enjoy, for your cichlids are certain to mesmerize you with their never-ending theatrical performance.

Swimming Society

Extending considerably further than the charismatic interaction with their keepers, cichlid intelligence is a major factor in their level of evolution and

Your cichlids are smart, and will come to recognize and love you—and the food your approach often promises!

socialization. Whether you keep a group of one species or several species together, you will observe interactions among the fishes that are constantly changing. If you watch very closely, you will note that no matter how docile or how aggressive the species, one fish always seems to be getting bullied by the others. Being the smart cichlid that it is, the harassed victim will learn to find and hover close to a safe hideaway. This is the low cichlid on the tank's social totem pole, which is topped by one who reigns supreme. Most likely, the high-ranking fish will be a male, and he must constantly prove his prowess in order to maintain his position and to attract the ladies in the aquarium.

Beyond the superior cichlid and the beleaguered cichlid, numerous other acts will be playing themselves

out among the rest of the group. If you have two groups of species, each group will have its own set of ranks and, depending on the species and your tank setup, will intermingle or remain aloof from the other species.

Heart and Mind

As you get to know your cichlids and they begin to spawn and raise their young, an entirely new story will unfold before your eyes. Closely observing the intelligence your fishes demonstrate by forming pairs and managing their fry is the nudge that inevitably pushes the casual cichlid keeper into the realm of the truly addicted. Varying in method from species to species, you will find an incredibly fascinating system of communication that will eventually lead a male and female to form a pair or, in the case of a harem spawner, one male to be the sole attractant to all the females in the tank.

When it comes to raising the fry, the picture becomes even more eye opening. Minute movements of a parent fish's body—a twitch of one pectoral fin, a flip of the tail, or a shimmy of the body—send a signal to the young. The different signals may convey any number of things, like telling the fry to follow the mother, or letting them know when and where to feed, to gather in safety, or that it is okay to spread out and forage.

Cichlids Come in all Sizes for all Spaces

No matter how much or how little space you have, there is sure to be a cichlid to fit your tank. When the length of a cichlid is measured from the tip of the nose to the tip of the tail, this measurement is known as the total length, or TL. When a fish is measured from the tip of the nose to the caudal peduncle (base of the tail), that measurement is known as the standard length, or SL.

Dwarf Cichlids

The smallest cichlids are under 3.5 inches (9cm) TL and are known as dwarf cichlids. Dwarf cichlids include numerous South American species, such as *Apistogramma, Biotoecus, Laetacara, Nannacara,* and *Mikrogeophagus*; West African cichlids, such as *Pelvicachromis*; and some of the African Rift Lake species, such as the smaller *Julidochromis* and the shell-dwelling lamprologines of Lake Tanganyika.

Your cichlid community will create a complex web of relationships. In time you'll come to understand them all.

Don't Swim So Close To Me

Some cichlids keep larger territories than others, which means you might need a bigger tank depending on the species you choose. As is always the case, research and accommodate the specific needs of the fish before buying them.

The minimum required space for a pair of dwarf cichlids is a tank 24 inches (61 cm) long, 12 inches (30 cm) wide, and 12 inches (30 cm) high—plus at least 8 inches (20 cm) more of head room for maintenance, which equals a total of 20 inches (51 cm) from the base of the tank to the ceiling of the area. A 15-gallon (57-l) aquarium will fit into this space. Ideally, you should provide your dwarf cichlids with a 20-gallon (76-l) long aquarium, which requires a space 30 inches (76 cm) long, 12 inches (30 cm) wide, and 20 inches (51 cm) high—12 inches (30 cm) of tank and 8 inches (20 cm) of extra head room.

Along with their size, dwarf cichlids are known for getting along with tankmates in an appropriately sized aquarium, when not in breeding mode. This trait makes them an excellent choice for newcomers.

Medium Cichlids

Next are the medium-size cichlids, which range from 3.5 to 6 inches (9 to 15 cm) TL. Thickness and body height will vary by species, but not as substantially as with the larger cichlids. Medium cichlids include numerous South and Central

Medium-size cichlids like Biotodoma cupido *need a tank at least 36 inches (91 cm) long and 18 inches (46 cm) wide.*

American species, such as *Aequidens*, *Biotodoma*, some *Crenicichla*, *Dicrossus*, *Archocentrus*, and *Cryptoheros*; African Rift Lake species, such as *Lamprologus* and Lake Victoria haplochromines; and many of the West African species, including the crater lake cichlids, such as *Konia* and *Tilapia*.

The minimum tank-space requirements for medium-size cichlids begin at 36 inches (91 cm) long, 12 inches (30 cm) wide, and 16 inches (41 cm) high, plus at least 8 inches (20 cm) more of head room for maintenance. These measurements are standard for 30-gallon (114-l) tanks, but you should consider a tank 18 inches (46 cm) wide instead. As you further understand the character of cichlids, you will see that this extra 6 inches (15 cm)

of width will make a great difference, for both you *and* your fish! So reserve a space 36 inches (91 cm) long, 18 inches (46 cm) wide, and 24 inches (61 cm) high for your medium cichlids. The tank that will fit into this space is known as a 40-gallon (151-l) breeder.

Large Cichlids

Our next category is the large cichlids, which range in size from 6 to 12 (15 to 30 cm) inches. Large cichlids include many of the South and Central American species, such as *Acarichthys*, *Astronotus*, some *Crenicichla*, *Geophagus*, *Pterophyllum*, *Symphysodon*, *Uaru*, *Thorichthys*, and *Amphilophus*, some of the African Rift Lake species, such as *Cyphotilapia*; and many of the Madagascar

Super-Sized

Cichlids that grow to over 12 inches (30 cm) in length are known as tankbusters. They're not for the faint of heart, or anyone with little free space. Tankbusters need *lots* of room! Included in this group are those cichlids from Central and South America such as *Nandopsis*, *Parachromis*, *Vieja*, *Cichla*, and *Hoplarchus*. To house these massive cichlids, you must have ample space—no less than 6 feet (2 m) long and 24 inches (61 cm) wide.

Cichlids

cichlids, such as *Paratilapia*, *Paretroplus*, *Ptychochromis*, and *Ptychochromoides*.

It will come as no surprise that large cichlids require large tanks, and not just because of their size! Close investigation into species's individual space requirements is a must. You may need only 4 feet (1 m) in length by 18 inches (46 cm) in width, as in a 75-gallon (284-l) tank, or you could easily go up to 6 feet (2 m) in length by 18 inches (46 cm) in width, as in a 125-gallon or 150-gallon (473-l or 568-l) tank.

Cichlids Come in all Colors and Shapes

The range of colors in cichlids is as spectacular as that of the rainbow! From the subdued loveliness of the hushed, natural tones of browns and creams, brushed with a soft teal and gold, the

appearance of *Neolamprologus multifasciatus* is punctuated by the striking baby-blue eyes that shimmer in direct contrast to the overall refined shades of this charming creature. On the other end of the spectrum are fish like the *Pelvicachromis* species, which sport breathtaking blends of blues, lavenders, and violets. Males bear a dorsal fin resplendent in reds, iridescent greens, and velvety blacks,

Oh, the Possibilities!

Not only do you have numerous sizes and colors to choose from, but cichlids also come in a variety of shapes as well! There are elongated, streamlined cichlids, such as *Cyathopharynx*, and thick, muscular cichlids, such as *Astronotus* (also known as oscars). There are oblong cichlids with rounded faces, such as the beautiful Lake Tanganyika *Tropheus*, and cichlids that are almost round, or disc-shaped, as in *Symphysodon* (also known as discus).

with a spangling of aqua; the abdomens of the females radiate a lovely red, melding perfectly into the lavenders and blues of the rest of the body.

Personality Plus!

A fish with personality? Cichlids have it all! Each species of cichlid has a distinctive character, and within the individual species, each fish will have its own personality. For example, most of the larger Central and South American species will easily become pets if housed by themselves, recognizing you when you appear and showing devout loyalty to you over any other person.

Chapter 2

Understanding
Cichlids

Members of the order Perciformes, which is made up of perch-like fishes, cichlids are of the family Cichlidae. There are visible characteristics that, when combined, differentiate cichlids from other fishes. Naturally, you will be looking for these outward signs first, but in setting up the optimum environment for your cichlids it is also important for you to understand the universal internal qualities by which scientists discern a cichlid.

Is It All About Looks?

The Lateral Line

Fishes have what is commonly known as a lateral line, which starts behind the operculum, or gill cover, and extends the entire length of the body to the caudal peduncle, or base of the tail. This lateral line is actually a narrow canal just under the scales that is made up of small holes, or sensory cells, connecting an underlying gel to the external surface of the fish's body. Transmitting extraneous sound and movement to the brain, these pores, as well as other single-cell sensory pores located in the head region and across the body, are extremely sensitive, detecting the slightest vibration in the water.

Whereas the lateral line of most fishes is continuous, the lateral line of cichlids is broken, or interrupted. On a cichlid, this line will begin behind the operculum, extending two-thirds to three-quarters of the way to the caudal peduncle, and come to an end. If you look below this, you will see that the lateral line starts up again and continues to the caudal peduncle.

Nostrils

Cichlids have one set of nostrils, rather than the two sets of most other fishes. One nostril is located on each side of the lower forehead, just above the mouth.

Fins

Both the dorsal and anal fins of a cichlid are single and continuous. They also begin, or lead, with individual spiny rays and then turn to soft branched rays.

Or Is It All in The Mind?

Intelligence

As we discussed in the previous chapter, cichlids exhibit a level of intelligence that ranks them among the most enjoyable and widely kept species of freshwater fishes.

Parental Behavior

Another major trait shared among cichlids, which we will discuss further in Chapter 8, is the demonstration of parental care for their eggs. Most species not only watch over the eggs but also continue to care for the fry for a time once they are free swimming, a characteristic most uncommon in other species of fishes and one that is of endless interest to their keepers.

SMALL FRY

Tap Dance, Not Glass

You should now understand and respect your cichlids' frustration and stress at having their aquarium glass tapped on. To the sensitive lateral line, it's much like having a drum pounded directly in your ears! Children (and adult visitors, too) will love to tap the glass to get your pets' attention, so try to discourage this behavior.

What We Don't See

Pharyngeal Jaw

The jaws of cichlids, as in other perciforms, have evolved over those of most other fishes to a sophisticated method of collecting and processing food. Most other fishes have one continuous jaw that must perform the dual job of collecting the food and what minimal chewing it is capable of before the food is sent to the esophagus. The distinctive pharyngeal jaws of cichlids divide a front set of jaws from a back set of jaws, offering the unique ability for the front and back jaws to function as separate units. The front set of jaws procures the food and sends it to the throat, where another set of jaws chews it.

Cichlids have developed specialized sets of jaws suited to their particular appetite—which often will include smaller tankmates.

Understanding Cichlids

The shape and size of the second jaw's teeth vary greatly from one species to another and identify what the cichlid feeds on. A mass of small, thin, pointed teeth is a good indication that the species eats planktonic algae, whereas long, thin teeth denote a piscivore, or fish eater. Large, thick teeth with flat tops are used for crushing foods such as mollusks or crustaceans. Some species have a combination of these types of teeth, which allows them to eat several types of food. When you keep cichlids in an aquarium, try to feed them whatever type of food is most appropriate to their physical makeup.

The Expert Knows

Other Notable Features

There are a few other features common to all cichlids. The opening of the intestine of most fishes is on the right side of the stomach, but the opening and first coil of cichlids' intestines are on the left side of the stomach. A line of fusion exists between each half of the lower pharyngeal bone. Also, within the construction of the ear there is a finite but notable difference from that of other fishes, and the eye socket has no bony shelf beneath it. Now you can wow all your friends with your thorough knowledge of cichlid anatomy!

Jaws of Life

The pharyngeal jaw has allowed cichlids the ability to adapt to many different types of habitats and to the food that is available. In severe conditions when less of their usual diet can be had, such as a prolonged drought, or in an area with intense competition for food, this second jaw has helped cichlids survive.

By understanding the pharyngeal jaw, you will have a better idea of what to feed your particular species of cichlid. Even though you do not directly see the pharyngeal jaw and teeth, research into what the species eats in its natural habitat will give you a good mental picture of the size and shape of your cichlid's teeth, and what foods to provide that are suitable for these teeth. It is best if cichlids are not forced to make major adaptations to our home aquariums that will affect the species over time, but rather that they be given the opportunity to exist and remain as they were meant to be in their natural habitat. Give those thick, flat teeth a few snails to crush, and let algae grow on the sides of your tank for your fine-toothed raspers to munch on!

Cichlids in Nature ... and in Your Aquarium

The cichlids of today evolved from their marine ancestors millions of years ago. This makes them secondary-division freshwater fishes, as opposed to modern-day primary-division freshwater fishes, which evolved from freshwater ancestors. Similarities are still found between cichlids and their marine forebears, as can be noted in the marine wrasses, damselfishes, and surfperches. Cichlids have a high salt tolerance and, from species to species, are able to adapt to a wide range of water conditions—a few even populate brackish-water habitats. Also, their reproductive pattern is not seasonal, but rather opportunistic, meaning that when they are properly conditioned with food to develop mature eggs, cichlids will breed at any time of the year, assuming the temperature is optimal.

Occupying a wide range of habitats, cichlids can be found throughout South America, Central America, both western and eastern Africa, Madagascar, and areas of Asia. They live in streams, rivers, floodplains, small ponds, and immense lakes, from still, quiet waters to rushing rapids and the bases of torrential waterfalls. The environment varies from region to region with substrates of sand, clay, mud, pebbles, stones, and huge boulders, and the water chemistry is as diverse in each habitat.

Many large male cichlids develop a nuchal hump, which is most prominent during the breeding season.

Starting Out

In Chapter 7, as you choose which species is best for you, you will research which habitat the cichlid of choice is from and see whether the chemistry of your tap water closely matches that of the water your cichlid inhabits in nature. Once you have become adept at keeping your first cichlids, you may keep different species and learn how to properly make natural adjustments to your water chemistry in order to mimic their native environment.

22

Water Chemistry

Understanding the impact water has on your cichlids is the single most important factor in determining your success in keeping cichlids. In contrast to the rich, vital, ever-changing water that cichlids inhabit in nature, the best that our home aquariums can offer is the same stale water that is both dined in and defecated in—hardly a palatable manner in which to live! The most significant thing that you can do to mimic the life-sustaining water of nature is to perform regular water changes.

Osmo-what?

Just as in human beings, the bodies of cichlids and other fishes are made up largely of water, which contains a certain amount of dissolved solids, or salts. But unlike humans, fishes are surrounded by water that also contains a certain amount of salts. The internal body fluids of the cichlid work with the water surrounding them to maintain a constant equilibrium of salts and fluids within and without. This system of checks and balances is known as osmoregulation.

The absolute most super-important key to caring for cichlids—and any other fish, for that matter—is providing them with fresh, clean water on a regular basis.

Soft-water cichlids like this *Apistogramma will often not breed successfully in hard water.*

Consider this. A cichlid's body contains a higher concentration of salt than does the fresh water that surrounds it. Because there is a greater amount of salt within the cichlid's body, this salt concentration is constantly drawing in the surrounding lower-salt fresh water, through both the gills and the semipermeable membrane of the skin—a process called osmosis. In turn, the fresh water seeks to leach some of the salt from the fish's body. Through osmoregulation, though, the fish retains the salts that its body needs and flushes out the excess fresh water in the form of urine.

The level of dissolved solids, or salts, in the natural water of cichlids varies from region to region. The soft water of the South American Amazonian cichlids contains low to trace levels of salts, while the hard water of the Rift Lake cichlids of Africa contains high levels

of salts. As the water passes through a soft-water South American cichlid, such as an *Apistogramma* or a discus, the osmotic pressure is greater than that on the Rift Lake cichlid because there is a greater ratio of salts in the body to salts in the water. A larger volume of water is pulled in, and the soft-water cichlid's system is designed to retain the required amount of salts from the low-salt water. If this same cichlid is placed in water that is higher in salts than its natural soft, low-salt water, its body will

Water World

Without osmoregulation, the low-salt water in which cichlids live would rob their bodies of salts and kill them. It would be like having the air we breathe stealing important chemicals from our own bodies.

For Your First Fish...

It is easiest to choose your first cichlid from those species that naturally inhabit water with a chemical composition similar to that of your tap water.

continue to work as it is accustomed to functioning to retain a high level of salts. But with so much salt available to retain, the excess salt will build up in the kidneys, which are ill-equipped for dealing with this, eventually causing damage and malfunction.

If, on the other hand, a cichlid from the Rift Lakes of Africa, such as a *Pseudotropheus demasoni* of Lake Malawi or a *Cyprichromis leptosoma* of Lake Tanganyika, is placed in water that is low in salts, the osmoregulatory system of this cichlid will not bring in enough salts if it works at its normal rate, so it will need to work double time if it is to draw the amount of salts from the water that the body requires. Both scenarios place undue stress on the osmoregulatory system of the cichlid, causing a gradual breakdown in the immune system leading to dysfunction and eventual disease.

In nature, cichlids live in water of immense volume with a constant turnover. Dissolved solids are dispersed, swept away by the currents, and seep into the earth. But in aquariums, dissolved solids will build up, reaching unmanageable levels for your cichlid's osmoregulatory system. As you have just learned, this excess buildup of dissolved solids will cause a gradual breakdown in your cichlid's immune system, leading to stress, dysfunctional kidneys, and eventual disease. So, what should you do? You need to remove water and replace it with fresh tap water on a regular basis. This simple matter of regular partial water changes, which we will discuss in depth in Chapter 4, is one easy and basic key to success with your cichlids.

Gills

We take breathing to supply our bodies with oxygen for granted because the air that surrounds us is replete with a high oxygen density. Cichlids of course need oxygen too, but water, on the other hand, has a very low concentration of oxygen. Gills have to extract oxygen from the water. When the mouth of the cichlid opens, water is drawn in, and when the mouth closes, the water is pushed back, where it rushes over the tiny lamellae of the gill arches. Oxygen is diffused into the bloodstream through these minute blood vessels, gas exchange occurs, and carbon dioxide is expelled through the lamellae and out of the gills.

Your cichlid's gills are extremely delicate and rank among the top three

> *This close-up shows the gills of a fish, rich in blood. These are extremely delicate tissues that are very susceptible to damage from dissolved wastes.*

areas of your cichlid that are most susceptible to damage from pathogens and poor water quality, the other two being the eyes and the mouth. Once again, in nature the water is under constant change, with no opportunity for toxic buildup of ammonia or nitrites, and has a huge surface area, which allows constant gas exchange and a fresh supply of dissolved oxygen to enter the water. But the opposite is true in aquariums. So what should you do to keep toxin levels low and oxygen levels high? Correct! You need to do regular water changes to mimic nature and keep the gills of your cichlids healthy and functioning optimally.

The Stress Factor

As you sat in front of your tank in Chapter 1 and observed your cichlids and the hierarchy they formed, you certainly worried for the cichlid that was the lowest on the totem pole and wished that there was something that you could do to assuage its fears. That cichlid's fears are actually well-founded; were it to be in the wild, it would have been able to retreat into the water's abyss, hide among piles of rocks, or scurry into the gnarled roots of the trees along the bank. These options are not possible in your aquarium because no matter where that fish tries to flee, there is always a glass wall, and, boom—its safety ends!

Stress is the number one killer of cichlids and other fishes. Just as in humans, stress is the root of innumerable illnesses. For fishes, there are many sources, such as harassment from bigger fishes, poor water quality, and extreme temperatures. Once you've determined what those sources are, you can rectify the problem and eliminate the stress.

Stop Bullying

Cichlids are notorious for their aggressive character, which stems from their territoriality and is part of the enjoyment and challenge of keeping them. Removing a persecuted cichlid seems like a good idea, but it will be meaningless (unless the fish is near death), since another cichlid will immediately be singled out and harassed. Instead, providing the victim with ample hiding places, like logs, rocks, clay pots, or PVC pipes, will assure it of security and offer great relief from its stress.

Check the Water

The very water that your cichlids live in can be another major cause of stress if it is not clean and within the parameters of the species that you are keeping. Constant low levels of ammonia, low levels of nitrites, a pH

Every fish in your aquarium should be provided with its own hiding places where it can escape harassment from tankmates.

Your fish will be forever grateful for the hidey holes you give them—especially since they can double as breeding grounds.

that is too high or too low, water that is too soft or too hard, or water that is too cold or too hot can seriously stress your fish. They might do all right for a while, but your cichlids will not have the shine and spark that they should.

If your cichlids look stressed and you are uncertain why, first check the temperature—cichlids generally prefer a range of 76° to 80°F (24° to 27°C), though this varies from species to species. Too much sun shining into your tank will cause overheating, and heaters can dangerously heat or chill your fish if they stick in the on position or fail to turn on. Be sure to place the aquarium where it won't get too much sunlight, and keep a second heater as a backup in case of emergencies.

If the temperature is as it should be, test the ammonia, nitrite, pH, and hardness levels. It is likely that you will find an abnormality here. Next, give your cichlids a refreshing water change and siphon the gravel. Chances are you will see a drastic transformation in the stress level of your cichlids!

Also, think about your aquarium husbandry practices—have you kept up with water changes, been overfeeding, cleaned the filter on schedule, or overcleaned the filter?

Natural Camouflage

PVC piping is a good place for a fish to hide, but it isn't aesthetically pleasing. Fortunately, you can let algae grow over it, which will help the pipe blend in and look more natural.

Or have you added any new item to the tank recently? When all other questions do not come up with the answer, it often turns out that a new piece of wood, rock, clay pot, or decoration brought in a contaminant. Try taking that item out and see whether things improve.

Peace and Quiet

An improperly located tank can also stress your fish. Cichlids like to see you face to face, or better yet, to look down on you. It's understandable that you probably don't want to have your cichlid aquarium above your head, but if it's at least above waist level, the fish will feel much more at ease when you or other people walk by. They also will be much more at ease if their tank is not directly in the flow of traffic through your home. Remember, to remain stress free your cichlids need to feel secure—so how about placing their aquarium up against a wall or in a corner, with enough room to place your easy chair right in front of the tank so that you can both enjoy each other's company?

Lights Out!

Just like you, your cichlids need the lights to go out at night so they too can sleep and wake up feeling well rested and stress free! So put the lights on a timer set to shut off at night.

Also, if your cichlids live with nocturnal species like catfishes, their different schedules can stress each other out. The cichlids might not get enough sleep if a nocturnal catfish is swimming about all night and pestering them from their sleeping quarters.

Survival of the Fittest

The will to survive is innate, and cichlids have accomplished this mission admirably for millions of years. The very essence of life for the cichlid in nature is to not be taken unawares by a lurking predator, to find food, to locate, attract, and procreate with a willing partner of the same species, and to make certain that their young remain safe, healthy, and growing. Time wasted in this precious cycle of life is simply unacceptable, and those who are fit for the task will be the ones who will carry on and uphold the species. Weak or lesser cichlids are not allowed into the spawning arena, and they therefore will not pass on their inadequate genes.

As you work with your cichlids, and wonder why they are behaving in a particular manner, be it aggression, territoriality, colors that go from vibrant to soft tones, or demonstrations of attentive parental care, keep this in mind, as more than likely they are practicing that which is instinctive to them—the survival of the fittest.

The Four Keys to Success with Cichlids

Along with a basic understanding of the nature of your cichlids, there are four major items of prime importance that will ensure your success.

1. Perform regular water changes!
● Enough cannot be said for maintaining a schedule of regular partial water changes, which we will elaborate on in Chapter 4. With a regimen of regular water changes, your cichlids will be certain to thrive!

2. Do not overfeed your cichlids!
● Most cichlids are gluttons, and they are all very good at putting on a puppy-dog face and begging for more food long after they have had enough. Overfeeding can cause health problems for your fishes and will quickly pollute your aquarium.

3. Do not overcrowd your cichlids!
● While there are a few special cases in which heavy stocking rates are used to manage aggression, it is best to provide the vast majority of cichlids with adequate space for their own territories. If you are unable to resist buying more cichlids, set up another aquarium; don't overload the one you have.

4. Care for your good bacteria!
● A properly functioning biological filter is your greatest ally in keeping your cichlids healthy. In the next two chapters we will discuss the importance of biofilter bacteria and how to properly care for these invisible workhorses.

Chapter 3

Preparing the
Cichlid
Aquarium

Now that you have a basic understanding of cichlids, you are ready to gather the equipment and supplies necessary for preparing your cichlid aquarium. This chapter will help you shop for and set up a safe, healthy, and enjoyable new home for your new friends.

Location, Location, Location

Determining where to place your cichlid aquarium is a major decision, and the first one to consider; once you have it set up, the likelihood of moving it in the future is slim. Therefore, make sure you have a space for it that both you and your cichlids are happy with, and where your cichlids can be most enjoyed.

Once the aquarium is filled with water it will be extremely heavy. Including substrate and decorations, the whole setup can weigh 10 pounds per gallon (more than a kilo per liter), which translates to a hefty 400 pounds (181 kg) just for that modest 40-gallon (151-l) tank we discussed earlier. In order to hold this weight, the floor must be solid and durable. The ground floor of any home or one with concrete underlying it is peferable. If the aquarium is over 50 gallons (189-l) and is to be on an upstairs floor, it is advisable to first have a professional check the structure of the house and make sure the floor can handle that kind of weight.

Considerations

Easy access to electricity is necessary, as you will need to use several outlets, all of which should be protected by ground-fault interrupting circuits. A close source of water and a drain will make your aquarium upkeep much easier. It is also essential that your tank be situated on a level floor; any tilt can cause a stress fracture in the glass. If the floor is not exactly level, adjustments will need to be made in the aquarium stand to correct this.

Windows

Placing your aquarium near a sunlit window will promote lush growths of generally unwanted algae and overheat the water, particularly in the summertime. If situating your tank near a window is your only choice, your cichlids will enjoy having an ample supply of filamentous algae to graze on and receiving plenty of healthy sunlight; you will just need to clean the tank more often and carefully maintain proper temperatures during warmer months. Also, you can

The Expert Knows

Water Falls

With all aquariums, as careful as you are, there is certain to be water spillage at one time or another. If the phone rings or the dog needs to be let out while you're changing the aquarium water, you can become distracted and end up with a drenched floor. A filter malfunction can also cause a major spill. With this in mind, be certain that your aquarium is not placed on your brand new oak flooring or luxurious wool carpet, with Grandma's favorite antique armoire sitting next to it. It's better to have waterproof linoleum as a base, and an area around the tank that will not be damaged if it gets wet.

Placing your tank near a window can brighten your tank, but the sunlight can create too much algal bloom and overheat the water.

always control the level of sunlight by closing the blinds or curtains on nearby windows.

Choosing the Tank

The rule of thumb when selecting the tank for your cichlids is to purchase the largest tank that you can afford and have room for. A 50- or 125-gallon (189- or 473-l) aquarium may sound absolutely overwhelming at first, so think of the tank in inches instead. How much space do your fish need? (Remember, we talked about this in the first chapter.) Describing a tank in inches also goes over much better when pleading with your spouse or parent for that first tank, or, "Just one more little tank, please—it will *only* take up 36 inches (or 91 cm)!" This sounds much more palatable than having to say "50 gallons (or 189 l)!"

From what you have learned about cichlid territoriality and their natural instinct for strong, defensive brood care, you now know that in order to thrive, cichlids need as much room as you can give them. In nature, they have virtually infinite room. Of course you cannot replicate this at home, but whatever you can do to give your cichlids space, the closer you will come to observing cichlid behavior as it occurs in nature—the boundaries of the aquarium will become less of

Fortress of Solitude

Above all, place the tank in a spot that isn't too busy or hectic but that will still allow you to hang out and spend time with your pets. This is most important of all, for you want to have a place to sit back, relax, and enjoy your cichlid aquarium!

The more fish you want, the larger the tank you'll need. With cichlids that can often mean an aquarium of 100 gallons (379 l) or more.

a factor in stifling their natural actions and rituals.

Also, as unusual as it may seem, aquariums actually become easier to take care of the bigger they are! Remember the huge volumes of water constantly flowing around your cichlids in nature? As the amount of water you provide your cichlids increases, the impact of human error, mechanical malfunction, and toxins like ammonia decreases. For example, if your heater gets stuck in the on position, it will heat the water and kill the fish in a 10-gallon (38-l) tank much faster than it could in a 50-gallon (189-l) tank. The same is true for the results of a power outage or a filter that has been left uncleaned.

Therefore, start with at least a 40-gallon (151-l) breeder tank, which is 36 inches (91 cm) long, 18 inches (46 cm) wide, and 16 inches (41 cm) high, or a 50-gallon (189-l) tank, which is 36 inches (91 cm) long, 18 inches (46 cm) wide, and 19 inches (48 cm) high. If you absolutely do not have this much space for a tank, try starting with a 20-gallon (76-l) tank, preferably a 20-gallon long, which is 30 inches (76 cm) long, 12 inches (30 cm) wide, and 12 inches (30 cm) high. Otherwise, go with a 20-gallon high, which is 24 inches (61 cm) long, 12 inches (30 cm) wide, and 16 inches (41 cm) high. Ten-gallon (38-l) tanks and smaller are best employed for raising fry or for use as you master the techniques of successful cichlid husbandry and water-change practices.

Once you have chosen which tank size you have space for, you can then begin to research the species that you would like to keep. If you do your research and decide that you would most like to start out with a cichlid that requires a larger tank than what you have room for, it is best to look now for a space to accommodate a larger tank, as you must have one that is suitable for the size of the fish as a full-grown adult before you purchase the fish!

To disperse their territorial nature, cichlids do best in an aquarium that has the greatest footprint that you can provide. In other words, a tank that is

Bigger is Better!

The larger the aquarium, the more stable and healthy it is likely to be. Think of it this way: if you mix a tablespoon of hot cocoa mix into a glass of milk, you'll notice a big change. But if you add that same tablespoon to a whole bottle of milk, it'll have a much smaller effect. It works the same way with unwanted waste in aquarium water.

16 inches (41 cm) wide is much preferable to one that is 12 inches (30 cm) wide. When a dominant cichlid goes on the chase of a subordinate cichlid, a 12-inch-wide (30-cm) tank gives the victim only a narrow corridor to flee down, and then suddenly it is up against the wall! Can you put yourself in its shoes (or fins)? Heading full tilt into that glass wall, with no place to go, right or left, and a big bully in the rear must be a terrible fright! The wider the area, the more turns the chase can take. Also, you have more room to place caves, logs, and pots and to devise other niches for quick escape. This is an excellent opportunity to exercise your creativity, working through one of the exciting challenges of keeping cichlids!

Glass or Acrylic?

When you arrive at the aquarium shop, you will be faced with the choice of a glass tank or an acrylic tank. Each of these has its pros and cons, and this will be a personal decision for you. One factor to take into consideration is that acrylic is lighter and will not break as easily. Acrylic also retains heat better than glass. On the other hand, acrylic will scratch, and it does cost more than glass. Glass aquariums do not tend to scratch unless treated roughly, and they are less expensive than acrylic. However, glass tanks break more easily, they tend to lose heat faster, they are heavier than acrylic, and there is a slight greenish tint, particularly in the thicker glass of large tanks. However, with greenery in the tank, this green tint will blend quite nicely into the natural appearance.

You don't have to go this far, but you'll want to provide your cichlids with the largest home you have room for and can manage.

Shapes

The aquarium shop will undoubtedly have a display of aquariums in a variety of shapes for you to select from. Traditional aquariums are in a rectangular shape, like those that we have been discussing. There will be many others to choose from, including hexagons, bow fronts, tall cylindrical shapes, and any number of other fashions—or fads, as they may be. In making your final decision, ask yourself whether what might look like a fun and novel aquarium now will still look so appealing to you sitting in your home months or years from now. Also, ask yourself whether it will be easy to maintain. Some tall aquariums, for example, might make it hard for you to

reach the bottom to clean. You want to enjoy the routine care of your cichlids and not have it become a difficult chore. Does the tank have ample surface area (which is important for gas exchange, which allows fish to breathe), and most importantly, is the tank one that meets the needs of your cichlids?

Choosing the Stand

The stand on which you place your cichlid aquarium will come down to a choice of deciding on whether you would like it to be decorative or purely functional. If your aquarium is in a more formal area of your home, such as the living room, there is a wide assortment of lovely wooden stands with cabinets underneath to discreetly house the filter and other maintenance equipment. The doors offer easy access for filter maintenance and room for a light to be mounted to help you see what you are doing. These stands come

given the array of equipment, supplies, and gadgetry. What do you need and what is excessive? While cichlidophiles do seem to share the common trait of being collectors of fish stuff—corners of their homes or basements piled high with tubing, parts, old equipment that no longer works, and new equipment that looked great in the shop but has yet to be put to use—you will have many purchases to make as you start out, so let's focus on what you actually will need. There is ample time to collect later.

The Filter

Cichlids have considerable body mass and consume food accordingly,

in several wood finishes, such as cherry, oak, and walnut, or they can be painted in a variety of hues.

If your cichlid aquarium is to be in a casual family room in the basement, say, and money is a consideration, there is no reason not to place it on a less expensive iron aquarium stand, which does not take up a lot of room, is level and strong, and quite often has a lower shelf for supplies—or your next aquarium! Always use a stand manufactured to hold the weight of the aquarium you have in order to avoid costly and possibly tragic accidents.

Selecting Equipment

Walking down the aisles of your local aquarium shop can be overwhelming,

Aquariums can come in some interesting shapes, so choose whatever you'll most like looking at and maintaining for a long time.

thus producing a lot of waste, which they expel into their water. A filter is the single most important piece of equipment that you will purchase and a must in helping to remove the impurities in the water caused by these wastes. On top of keeping your cichlid's water clean, a filter provides the circulation necessary to allow the maximum exchange between oxygen and carbon dioxide at the water's surface.

There are three types of filtration: mechanical, biological, and chemical. Some filters perform one type, some perform two, and some perform all three. Let's take a look at each task individually to understand what filtration is really all about.

Mechanical Filtration

Mechanical filtration removes the particulate matter in the aquarium, such as excrement, uneaten food, and old vegetation from aquatic plants, down to the tiny materials that, if left unfiltered, the eye sees only as a cloud in the water. These particles are captured as the water is passed through a sponge or floss medium while the water continues on its course through the filter and back into the aquarium.

Biological Filtration

Biological filtration is the most important filtration of all, and actually understanding biological filtration will prove helpful to you in implementing the four keys to success with your cichlids. Biological filtration can seem overwhelmingly complicated, but it isn't at all!

Bacteria may at first sound like a bad thing, but a few types of bacteria are crucial to the health of your cichlids, and to your success as a cichlid keeper. Let's call them the good bacteria. Your cichlids are continually producing ammonia and expelling it into the very water in which they live. In nature, as you now know, this ammonia would be dissipated and swept away into the huge volumes of water, taken care of by nature's grand nitrogen cycle, and the gills and body of the cichlids living therein would have no contact with it. In our home aquariums, it is a totally

Cichlids

Many aquarium stands are designed to look attractive and conveniently hide filters and other unsightly equipment.

Porous rock and driftwood provide more surface area for good bacteria than other types of decorations.

different picture. But help is on the way, as good bacteria eat ammonia!

Once the good bacteria consume the ammonia, they expel it as nitrites. Unfortunately nitrites are also toxic to cichlids and other fishes, but another type of good bacteria eats the nitrites, expelling them as nitrates, which are not harmful to your cichlids unless they build up to intolerable levels. Your regular water changes will prevent that from happening. And for some more good news, the good bacteria that consume ammonia and the good bacteria that consume nitrites live together!

In order to achieve the large masses of good bacteria necessary, large areas must be provided for them to form on. The greater the surface area provided, the more good bacteria will grow. Good bacteria also need water and dissolved oxygen to survive—just like your cichlids! Porous materials such as sponges and lava rocks are excellent choices for providing your good bacteria with abundant surface area. Some biological-filter materials, like bioballs, are manufactured with the explicit purpose of providing the greatest surface area possible in a small space.

The More the Merrier

So we want as many good bacteria as can possibly fit into our cichlid aquarium. Where do good bacteria grow? Once started and if taken care of properly (see Chapter 4), good bacteria grow on every surface imaginable, covering the substrate, walls, rocks, pots, and any other decor, as well as on the media contained within the filter. You need a lot of good bacteria to keep up with devouring all the ammonia and nitrites, as a zero level must be maintained in the aquarium.

Chemical Filtration

Chemical filtration removes unwanted substances from the water by chemical means. The most common chemical filtration medium is activated carbon, which adsorbs a great number of impurities, but resins are available to remove other specific contaminants, such as phosphate or ammonia. Many people feel that chemical filtration is important and that it reduces the need for water changes. Carbon filtration will certainly clarify yellow-tinted water, which gives the impression that the water is clean. It cannot, however, remove all the pollutants in the water. By making the water look cleaner, chemical filtration might convince an aquarist to change water less frequently, but don't forget about those invisible wastes and impurities!

Another consideration is that the useful life of activated carbon is quite short—often less than two weeks. Many aquarists who use carbon and swear by it are actually giving it credit where none is due. Unless the carbon is replaced regularly and with great frequency, its ability to adsorb pollutants is actually maxed out, and its only contribution is to biofiltration, since activated carbon is one

Keep a Backup

It is a good idea to keep more than one filter in your cichlid aquarium. Choose a filter that handles all three functions, and a second one for extra biological filtration.

of the most porous substances you can use in a biofilter.

If you wish to use it, chemical filtration can make your aquarium water extra clean, but do not rely on it to perform magical feats of waste removal. And rest assured that you can raise healthy, thriving cichlids for years on end without using any chemical filtration at all.

Filter Choices

A wide variety of filter choices is available in today's market. Some of them are quite basic and utilize only one means of filtration, where others combine more than one. There are two considerations to keep in mind when choosing a filter. First, you want a filter that can keep up with the large amount of waste produced by cichlids, with abundant

40

Cichlids

Water Changes Win Every Time

Chemical filtration is a wonderful application of technology, and it can purify water in the aquarium. It cannot, however, take the place of proper husbandry, which will prevent many impurities from accumulating in the first place, or proper water changes, which will remove not only the impurities that chemical filtration removes but also the impurities it will not remove.

surface area for colonization by good bacteria. Second, choose a filter that you will look forward to maintaining and that is not so complicated that you will dread cleaning it. If you dread cleaning the filter, that filter is not the right choice for you. When a salesperson makes a filter sound good, be certain that you take it out of the box, hold it in your own hands, try to open it by yourself, take apart and replace the inside, and close it back up. Then picture this same filter filled with water and caked with algae and slime. Now, ask yourself whether this is a filter that you can work with. If the answer is yes, then it is the filter for you!

Internal Filters

An internal filter sits inside the aquarium and can be a simple air-driven filter, or one driven by a motor. A box filter allows you to insert the medium of choice, performing one, two, or all three forms of filtration. Sponge filters are excellent for holding large amounts of good bacteria and are easy to maintain. Several of them can be kept in one tank. You can never have too many sponge filters, and they provide a great means of backup.

A motor-driven internal filter will oftentimes be fitted with a sponge, or have a cartridge with floss and carbon that can be removed, disposed of, and replaced.

Hanging Filters

The hang-on external filter comes in many variations and is an excellent

Some filters are designed to hold biological-filter media known as bioballs, which provide large amounts of surface area on which good bacteria can grow.

choice for performance and ease of maintenance. One type of outside hang-on filter has a cartridge with floss and carbon that can be removed, disposed of, and replaced. If you choose a filter with a disposable cartridge, it is advisable to have at least one other source of biological filtration, such as a sponge or two—when you dispose of the cartridge, you will also be throwing out much of your bacteria!

Canister Filters

A canister filter sits underneath or beside the aquarium (or hidden from

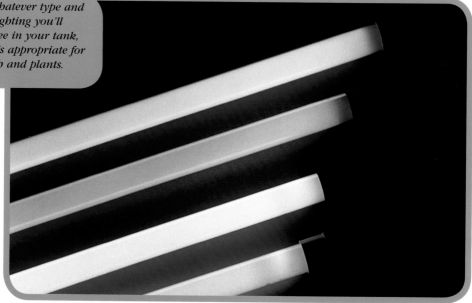

Choose whatever type and color of lighting you'll want to see in your tank, as long it's appropriate for all the fish and plants.

view in many aquarium stands) and offers compartments for several types of media. These filters typically have powerful water pumps, and because the water is forced through the media under pressure, they are very effective filters. Canister filters are very efficient and do not need to be cleaned as often as the others. However, unless it is made in an easy-to-access, easy-to-restart design, you might not enjoy cleaning a canister filter when it does need it.

Wet/Dry Filters

Although there are smaller versions that hang over the back of the tank, the wet/dry filter typically sits underneath the aquarium and is a very effective filter for the cichlid aquarium. Enough cannot be said for the biological filtration that a wet/dry filter will provide for your cichlids. Water is run from the tank through a layer of floss to capture particulate matter, then continues in a constant stream over bioballs, which will be colonized by bacteria. The water may then be passed through other forms of filtration, or simply sent on its way and returned to the tank. The wet/dry filter is an excellent choice of filtration for your cichlids, particularly the larger species, which produce more waste than others.

Lighting

The sun-filled days of summer find many cichlid keepers placing their fish outside in ponds, tubs, and other appropriate vessels. Their growth and vitality in the summer months, not to mention their productivity, is astonishing. The sun plays a significant role in those results and certainly makes lighting worth close consideration.

The sun's rays are responsible for allowing the body to utilize various ingested vitamins and minerals once ingested. Thanks to modern technology, many light bulbs emulate the light of the sun's rays, and they are the next best thing to actual sunlight.

When choosing lighting, keep in mind that your cichlids will not be comfortable in constant total illumination. Even those outdoor tubs have floating leaves and logs under which to find security and shade. Unless you are also lighting for plants, use only one bulb, and provide areas of shadow within the tank, as most cichlids are at ease if able to come and go from the light as they please, just as they do in nature. Remember, the more secure your cichlids feel, the more you will enjoy seeing them.

As for the length of time to light your cichlid tank, setting your timers to mimic nature is an easy and foolproof method—10 to 12 hours of light per day is perfect. Proper lighting will make your cichlids feel and look their best!

Heaters

Cichlids live in a range of water temperatures, varying from species to species. However, for general cichlid maintenance, an appropriate temperature range is 76° to 80°F (24° to 27°C). Submersible heaters are available with a dial for easy temperature adjustment, and come in wattages of 50 to 300. The package will have a chart to guide you as to how many watts you need for the size of your tank. In aquaria over 50 gallons (189-l), it is a good idea to use more than one heater, each of them less than the required amount of watts for the tank. This way, if one heater becomes stuck in the on position, as can happen, it will not be able to heat the water enough to harm the fish. Or if one heater ceases to work, the alternate heater will at least maintain the heat at a tolerable level until you notice that the other heater is broken. Also, a backup heater is always a good idea to have on hand, and an annual replacement of all heaters is a widely exercised and sensible practice.

Protect the Heater

Larger cichlids are likely to stake out their territory by doing their best to demolish any internal aquarium equipment, often resulting in a shattered heater. This can be avoided by placing the heater in the sump of a wet/dry filter, where it will heat the water as it passes through the filter. If you must leave the heater in the aquarium, glue a piece of acrylic with numerous holes drilled into it to each side of a corner of the tank with aquarium glue before filling the tank with water. You can insert the heater into this triangular compartment and suction-cup it to the side of the tank.

Thermometers

Of course, you can only know the temperature of the aquarium by using a thermometer. There are several thermometers to choose from, one being the popular flat stick-on variety that is easy to read and can be placed unobtrusively on the front or a side of the aquarium. It is a good idea to place this in the center of the water column, as opposed to a corner. Like placing a thermometer in the center of a roasting turkey, putting your thermometer near the center of the water column will give you the most accurate reading.

Tank Lid

Cichlids are known to leap out of the water, oftentimes as a last resort when chased by another, or sometimes just in sheer jubilation. Needless to say, fish do not fare well on the floor, and it will be quite an upsetting experience for you to discover one in this avoidable predicament. A tight-fitting cover on your cichlid aquarium is essential. Be certain that there are no spaces big enough for one of your cichlids to jump through along the front, back, or edges—you would be amazed by how tiny an opening cichlids are able to propel themselves through!

Other Equipment and Supplies

It is a good idea to have at least two plastic buckets that are used exclusively for your cichlid aquarium. Label these with a waterproof marker with something like "Cichlids Only!" to be certain that they are not mistaken for a household bucket and used for detergents or other cleaning. A water-changing siphon of course is essential. Other important basic items include a few soft nets of varying sizes, a sponge intended for aquarium use, and a dipper of some sort, such as an empty cylindrical plastic bird-food or yogurt container. From here, as with any true cichlidophile, your collection of fish stuff is certain to grow!

Thermometers can be simple submerged types or more complicated hang-on types, but they are an absolute must in any aquarium.

Substrate & Aquascaping

You may choose to place gravel or sand on the floor of the aquarium, or you may wish to leave the bottom bare. Whichever you decide to do, it is a good idea to first paint the bottom of your tank (on the outside!) with a flat, dark paint, such as a deep green. Cichlids will feel more secure without the reflections from the glass. And even with a substrate placed on the bottom, the cichlids can dig and expose the glass, so it's best to paint it. The deep green is also aesthetically pleasing for the overall appearance of the aquarium, rather than seeing what is underneath the tank through an unpainted bottom.

If you decide to add substrate, be aware that certain species of cichlids prefer sand—some actually sift it through their mouth and gills to obtain food—and some do well with gravel. A coarse-grained sand is better than a fine-grained, as it allows more room for water flow to penetrate between and around the grains. Gravel is also available in various sizes and colors. You may choose to use all one size, or place a base of one size and scatter a small amount of a larger size on top. The colors can also be mixed. If you enjoy a natural look, a selection of neutral tones is attractive. Crushed glass is not an acceptable substrate!

Many cichlids root around in the substrate, so it's often safer to provide sand or gravel instead of sharp or large rocks.

The back wall of the aquarium is best if painted on the outside or covered with a commercially produced background, most of swhich depict realistic planted or rocky scenes. This will avoid spooking from reflections, and will give the cichlids a sense of security in the knowledge that at least one side is safe from predators that might be lurking in the shadows outside the tank's walls.

Cichlids do best with ample places to choose from to declare as their territory and to hide in. The more nooks and crannies that you can provide them with, the less they will be terrorized by each other, and the more you will see them out and about, as the happier they will be. Wood, rocks, clay pots with the bottoms cut out, plants in pots, plastic plants, PVC piping, and a wide array of commercially made decor from your local aquarium shop will do nicely.

A Point on Plants

There are actually very few plants in the substrate of most cichlid habitats aside from those that are growing along the banks and become submerged during the rainy season in some areas. There are, however, grasses and plants that overhang into the water from the edges of some streams, rivers, and lakes, and many regions contain fallen decomposing leaves. Many cichlids can be found spawning and with their broods of fry up along the edges of these banks in the more shallow waters, as the vegetation is ideal for the safety of their young as well as providing an abundant and nourishing first food source, so you might want to add some floating or overhanging plants to your aquarium. Certain species of cichlids eat or destroy plants, making the addition of aquatic vegetation to the home aquarium a rather costly proposition. But plants such as *Anubias* and Java fern, whose roots do not need to be submerged in substrate, are excellent choices for a cichlid aquarium.

Putting It All Together

Place the aquarium on its stand and double check that it is completely level. Place the substrate in, hook up the filter, and position the light. Arrange any rocks or driftwood you are using as decor. Next, fill the tank with water and add dechloraminator as necessary. You can prevent the stream of water from demolishing your aquascaping by setting a bowl or pitcher in the tank; pour the water into this vessel and allow it to overflow into the tank.

Set up your heater and plug it in. Start up the filter. Let everything run for at least 24 hours to make sure the temperature remains steady and the filtration is working properly. Now you may think you're ready to add your fish, but not so fast! Remember those good bacteria? It takes time for them to grow, and when you start out with a new tank, there isn't any biofilter at all. So what do you do?

Cycling

You will hear a great deal about "cycling" an aquarium, and much of it will be contradictory. What you need to know is that cycling refers to establishing the necessary part of the nitrogen cycle in your tank—in other words, maturing the biofilter. There are many ways of cycling a tank, and some are better than others. Many involve using a few small fish as the ammonia source to start the bacteria growing, then gradually adding more fish as the filter matures. This method has its own problems, but since many cichlids are large, heavy-bodied fish that produce a lot of wastes, it is especially problematic with a cichlid tank. Fortunately, there is a better, easier way of getting a mature biofilter for your new setup: beg, borrow, or steal one!

If you already have one or more aquariums, you can do this by yourself. If not, you'll have to enlist the assistance of another aquarist or a friendly retailer. Since "cycling a tank" means producing a mature biofilter, you can have an instantly cycled tank by installing an already mature biofilter. There are several ways of accomplishing this.

Splitting a Biofilter

If you choose a power filter that has modular media that you can remove and replace, you can take half the media (sponges, floss, or biowheels) from a power filter on an established aquarium. The concern here is that the

With a little imagination, anything from clay pots to PVC pipes can add flair to your tank, as long as whatever you add won't leach unwanted chemicals into the water.

Cichlids

Cichlids Like Redecorating

However you decide to decorate your cichlid aquarium, carry on with the knowledge that no matter what your ideas of a beautiful arrangement may be, your cichlids will be certain to have a different view, and take every opportunity to jubilantly rearrange the fruits of your labor! So don't be too surprised or upset when you visit your tank one morning and find overturned decor everywhere.

large cichlids is an excellent choice. The only drawback here is that you have to do this four to six weeks before you want to set up your new aquarium. Simply let the filter run all this time, then unplug it, install it on your new tank, and plug it back in. Instant cycling! As in the previous case, you will be removing some of the biofilter from the original tank, and the new biofilter may or may not be up to the task of neutralizing all

established tank must not be overcrowded, since it will be losing half its biofiltration capacity. You must also be careful not to tax the new filter by heavily stocking that tank, since it does not yet have a full complement of bacteria. Both tanks need to be monitored for a while to make sure there isn't a dangerous rise in ammonia or nitrite, but usually all will be well.

Maturing the Filter in Advance

Another option is to take your new filter and install it on an established aquarium—preferably a messy, crowded one. A tank housing several

Keep A Little Extra

A common practice among cichlidophiles with rooms of dozens of tanks is to keep extra sponge filters bubbling away in several of their large aquariums full of big cichlids. Any time they want to set up a new tank, they remove one of these sponge filters, place it into the new setup, and add the fish. You hardly need dozens of tanks to be prepared, though. You can keep an extra filter running on your first aquarium in anticipation of someday starting a second one.

the wastes in the new tank, so both aquariums should be monitored for at least several days to make sure there is no appreciable rise in ammonia or nitrite.

Up and Running

Whether you borrow a biofilter or mature one in a more traditional cycling procedure, you will come to the point that ammonia and nitrite routinely test at zero, and nitrates are beginning to accumulate in the water. Congratulations! You have established a cichlid tank. Now all you have to do is take good care of your cichlids and the biofilter. Fortunately, their needs are much the same: good food, plenty of clean water, and proper temperature.

Once you've set up your tank and the heater and filter are running, it is time to begin cycling.

Chapter 4

Water Changes!

And Other Maintenance

As you now thoroughly understand, the water surrounding your cichlids is constantly flowing into and out of their bodies, and maintaining good water quality is the single most important factor in managing a healthy and vibrant cichlid aquarium. Water changes are the key to success.

What Makes Water Changes So Important?

Our cichlids in their natural environment have massive volumes of water surrounding them that is in constant change. Cichlids in our home aquariums are confined in minuscule amounts of water into which urine and excrement are constantly being expelled, and in which harmful toxins build up. Filters perform their job in excellent fashion, but there is no substitute for getting the water out of the tank and replenishing it with fresh water. The ultimate cichlid aquarium would have a hole in the bottom through which water was constantly draining out, and a hole in the top through which fresh water was constantly pouring in. Can you imagine how wonderful your cichlids would feel? Well, the more that you can replicate nature by way of regular water changes, the better your cichlids will feel!

The traditional ideology of changing 20 percent every two weeks simply does not come close to what is necessary to create this ultimate goal of constant change. The more water changed, more often, the better! A daily change of at least 60 percent of the water, preferably more, would be closing in on ideal. If once a week is all that you can manage, change at least 60 percent. If you already have a cichlid aquarium and are not managing it this attentively, change more water more often, gradually increasing the amounts and frequency in increments to adjust your fish to the new regimen. They will be glad that you did!

How to do a Water Change

An excellent tool for aquarists to use is a simple water changer that serves as a two-way conduit between the sink and

In nature, fish enjoy constantly changing water, but in aquariums, their water is only as fresh as you're willing to keep it.

The Most Important Key to Success!

Nothing matters more to the health of your cichlids, and indeed of all fish, than regular, proper water changes. Other maintenance is important too, but nothing trumps changing water!

a tank. By turning on the faucet, water is drawn out of the tank and right down the drain. When the tank has been emptied to the desired level, a twist of a connector reverses the flow, and fresh tap water fills up the aquarium.

It is important to make certain that the water refilling the tank is of the same temperature as that which is already in the tank. Do not fret over this, but simply hold your hand under the water going into the tank and then immerse the same hand in the water that is already in the tank. If an adjustment is needed, go to the sink and modify the temperature accordingly. Unless you have well water, pour a water conditioner that removes chlorine/chloramine directly into the stream of water entering the tank, or across the top of the tank water as it refills. If you are uncertain as to whether your municipal water

supply contains chloramines, use a water conditioner that removes both chlorine and chloramines.

The one concern of using the commercial faucet water changer is that a large amount of water is wasted as it goes down the sink along with the old tank water. A solution is to turn the faucet on, start up the siphon, and shut the faucet off once the water is running out of the tank and into the sink. As long as the water level in the tank is higher than the sink, the water will continue to drain from the tank, albeit more slowly than if the faucet were left running. Another solution is to attach a submersible pump to the end of the siphon that goes in the tank. The other end of the siphon tubing can go out the window and into the garden, or it can once again attach to your sink faucet. If you do choose to attach it to your sink faucet, when the

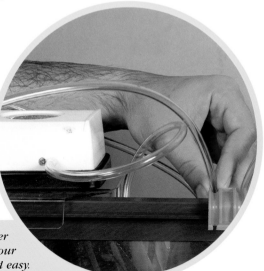

Tools like air pumps and water changers help make maintaining your aquarium relatively quick and easy.

Low-Tech Water Changing

A siphon and bucket can be used to change your water. However, changing water with this method is a recipe for turning the water change into a dreaded task, which will cause you to skimp on the chore, particularly with a large cichlid aquarium. Start out with the faucet water-change system and you will find it much easier to keep up with this vital part of aquarium maintenance.

tank is drained to the desired level, just turn the faucet on; as with the previous method, your tank will refill.

Water Changes are Easy, Enjoyable, and Rewarding!

For all the time that you spend with your cichlids, the water change can be among the most relaxing and rewarding of experiences. You will often find that your cichlids will see the siphon coming and rush out with eagerness to enjoy their fresh water. If you take this time

to place your hand down in the water, holding the siphon or resting on the bottom of the tank, oftentimes they will come up and nibble and poke at your fingers in gentle play.

When the new water begins to rush in, your cichlids will be ecstatic! A transformation will take place before your very eyes as their sides shimmer and they revel in the fresh water. There is nothing like the enjoyment and reward of giving your cichlids their water change! And to think that this much fun is the main key to success with the cichlid aquarium!

Cleaning the Gravel

The gravel or sand in your aquarium will accumulate debris that the filter does not take out, such as excrement and uneaten food. If you feed your fish properly, there is no reason to have uneaten food in the gravel, but this will be the end result of even an occasional overfeeding. In any case, there will be a lot of detritus among the gravel. A good time to clean the gravel is while you are changing the water. Of course, if you see chunks of food resting on the gravel an hour after you have fed your fish, you must take them out at that time.

The end of the water changer has a wide stiff plastic tube on the end. When you siphon the water out of the tank, place this tube down into the gravel. The gravel, along with the debris, will come halfway up the tube; the gravel then falls back to the bottom due to its weight, and the debris comes right up the siphon and out into the sink. Work around the wood, rocks, and other decor as best as you can, and up along the edges of the tank.

Regular Maintenance

The day-to-day maintenance of your cichlid aquarium is really not difficult, and some people regard it as a rejuvenating retreat from today's hectic lifestyle. The first thing you need to do, which will soon become second nature to you, is to take a look at each of the inhabitants of the tank. This takes only a moment and can tell you at once whether there is a problem that needs immediate attention or whether all is well within the aquarium. If the cichlids rush out for their expected meal, you can be quite certain that the aquarium is functioning as it should be. In Chapter 6 we will discuss steps to take if you do see a problem among the residents.

A quick glance at the thermometer on the tank is always a good idea. Get into the habit of placing your hand on

You can clean your substrate easily using a simple gravel-cleaning attachment at the end of your siphon when doing a water change.

the aquarium glass. You will soon come to know whether the water in the tank is of the correct temperature. If a heater has malfunctioned overnight, it is best to catch it in the morning rather than to walk in after work to a disaster that could have been averted.

Run your eyes over the filter to be certain that it is running properly just in case the intake or outflow

Your fish will never be happier than when that fresh water starts hitting their tank.

pieces were knocked off by an overly ambitious cichlid, or possibly a large piece of debris that might cause a problem during the day has become lodged in the mechanism.

Once you know that all is in good working order, your cichlids will be thrilled to receive their morning meal! If you are performing daily water changes, give your fish time to finish up breakfast and then bring out the siphon!

Filter Care

Taking Care of Your Good Bacteria

Take care of your good bacteria and they will take care of your cichlids! If you are to think of and manage your biofilter just as you do your cichlids, you will be a successful cichlid keeper. If the water is too hot for your cichlids, it is too hot for your good bacteria. If the water is too cold for your cichlids, it is too cold for your good bacteria. If you do not dechlorinate the water when adding new water from the tap, you will harm your cichlids, and you will harm your good bacteria. If you add chemicals or medications to the tank, some will kill your cichlids, and some will kill your bacteria. If the oxygen supply is cut off, your

cichlids will succumb, and so will your good bacteria.

You have worked diligently and done a great job in culturing your good bacteria, allowing them to accumulate on the tank sides and decor and cultivating them in the sponges and other media of your filters. Filters and sponges need to be cleaned, but some gunk is not a bad thing! Gunk is loaded with good bacteria. A squeaky clean tank with sparkling sides—and worse, an immaculate filter—is not necessarily a healthy tank, but rather one that has no good bacteria and is just waiting to be overrun by toxic ammonia!

Don't go overboard when cleaning your filters. A squeaky-clean filter is a filter devoid of the good bacteria your aquarium needs.

Your fish enjoy eating it, so some algae in your tank is good. Just don't let it coat the front glass or the aquarium will look grimy.

Rinse your bacteria-laden sponges in a bucket with aquarium water. Using the same water as that from which they came avoids shock to the good bacteria, and you can be certain that the rinse water contains no chlorine. Be gentle, and leave some of the dirt in the sponges. Rinse only one-half of your biological filter medium per cleaning, and alternate cleanings. This will allow the bacteria that have been disturbed to regenerate on the clean sponges, and the gunk-filled, good-bacteria-saturated sponges that are left in the tank will handle the ammonia and nitrites until the good bacteria on the clean sponge catch back up.

Make Nice With Bacteria

Treat your good bacteria with as much care as you do your cichlids, and you will have mastered one of the four keys to successful cichlid husbandry!

Cleaning Those Filters

The filters will need to be cleaned about once every month. Keep a chart or notebook beside the aquarium and jot down the date, what tasks you performed, and which filter was cleaned. If you are doing water testing, this is a good time to take note of the results so you can refer back to them in the future.

Mechanical filtration is only as good as its upkeep, since materials that are left in the filter, particularly uneaten food, will decay. The good bacteria will be able to handle some of this, but the breakdown of a large amount of excess food, or a dead fish, will produce more toxic ammonia than the good bacteria can manage at one time, and the toxins will soon be expelled back into the water, defeating the filter's purpose. Furthermore, if left uncleaned the filter medium will get plugged and water won't be able to flow through it.

As previously mentioned, sponge filters should be rinsed in a bucket of water that has been taken from the

Beware Overfeeding

The eyes of your cichlids are much larger than their stomachs, so beware that you are not taken in by their wanting looks and beguiling charm. In the wild, cichlids are opportunistic feeders, taking advantage of food when it is available and picking through what they can find when there is little. There is no such thing as two or three set meals per day at exactly the same hour, each filled with precisely measured protein, fats, carbohydrates, vitamins, and minerals. So don't overfeed them!

aquarium. You can easily obtain this water with the plastic dipper that you have gathered with your supplies. This dipper will be quite the useful tool, and you will find yourself relying on it for a variety of jobs, maybe one day even to move tiny fry! If you have more than one sponge, rinse only one per cleaning, and then rinse the other one during the next cleaning session.

Filters with a cartridge need to have the cartridge taken out, disposed of, and replaced by a new cartridge that has first been run under water. Remember to keep in mind that when you throw the old cartridge out, you are throwing out the good bacteria that you want in the aquarium. To mitigate the consequences of disposing of your tank's good bacteria, clean only one filter at a time, save the other filter for another week, and if there

are two cartridges, save the cleaning of the other cartridge for another week.

Algae Are Good!

Your cichlids will enjoy grazing on the algae that grow on the sides of the aquarium. Some cichlids spend their days in the wild eating the algae that cover the rocks, and in fact this can be a major food source. Since you want to be able to enjoy your cichlids, though, you probably will not wish to have so many algae that you are not able to see into the tank. Using your aquarium sponge, wipe down the algae on the front pane of glass, and allow the back and sides to take on the natural look of lush greenery. This is the perfect compromise—you can enjoy your cichlids, and they will enjoy their greens.

Feeding

One of the greatest charms of cichlids is their manner of communicating with us, winning our hearts and even taking on the qualities of the most devoted of pets! Feeding time, not surprisingly, is an opportunity to witness, or take part in, a particularly irresistible display of affection—remember, cichlids are smart!

Aquarium cichlids grow much larger in the domestic environment than their wild forebears, due to the plethora of rich foods that we give them. Unfortunately, this is not all good, because cichlids are often found to have unhealthy organs filled with fats from the overindulgence of our well-intended feedings. Sparse feeding and lean cichlids are a good thing!

Water Tests

There are several kits available for testing your aquarium water. You can easily find out whether the water in your cichlid aquarium contains toxic ammonia, toxic nitrites, or nitrates. Once your cichlid aquarium is established, a weekly check of the ammonia and nitrites is a good idea. You can jot the date and results in your notebook to refer to later. There should be zero ammonia and zero nitrites. Anything above this is simply unacceptable. If any ammonia or nitrites exist, you must do a water change immediately and re-examine your husbandry practices, particularly addressing the following four questions.

1) Has the tank been overfed?

2) Are there too many fish in the tank?

3) Have you taken diligent care of the good bacteria?

4) Have you kept up with your water changes?

Sound familiar? As long as you adhere to the four keys to success, there will be no ammonia or nitrites in your cichlid aquarium.

Two or three tiny meals per day is better than one large feeding. When you place the food into the aquarium, stand back and watch what is occurring in the tank. If the food is billowing about in clouds and settling on the bottom, it is simply way too much food! It will soon be lost in the crevices and crannies of the gravel and decor, where it will decompose and emit toxic ammonia. When you place food in the tank of large cichlids, there is no reason that any food should make it to the bottom of the tank, so watch what you are doing. Place in a few tablets, or whatever you are feeding, and let the fish eat it—it will go fast. When they are finished swallowing, place a few more on the surface of the water, and stand back again. Nothing will hit the bottom of the tank, and there will be no food to decay on the bottom of your cichlid aquarium. Okay—that is enough food for now!

59

Remember—Change the Water!

Nothing is more important than water changes! I cannot ever stress that enough. (But I'll sure try!)

Chapter 5

The Cichlid Diet

In most instances, cichlids in nature have a wide variety of foods to pick and choose from. Aside from the algae that grow within the tank, the residents of our home aquariums are confined to eating whatever we choose to offer.

F ollowing are five food groups that will provide a good basis for a well-rounded and healthy diet for your cichlids, especially if your feeding regimen is designed around the use of a few choices within each of the groups. The primary elements that you want to be aware of are protein, carbohydrates, fats, vitamins, and minerals.

Prepared Foods

With modern knowledge, feeding our cichlids has become much more of a science than it was 30 or more years ago, so the informed hobbyist now can be much more discerning when making his or her selection. Therefore, the enterprise of selling prepared foods is highly competitive, with the market carrying an extensive range of high-quality commercial foods in a wide variety of options suitable for the many species. From flakes and wafers to pellets of all sizes, both floating and sinking, you will find numerous prepared foods that are appropriate for the cichlids that you are keeping.

What to Look For

Many aquarists opt for high-protein food, but you should research the diet of the species of choice, as many cichlids are unable to effectively digest immense doses of protein condensed into one meal. Instead,

the natural diet of numerous cichlids consists of a substantial amount—often 85 percent or more—of roughage, or vegetable matter. Many prepared foods contain all vegetable matter in the form of a flake or a sinking wafer. Unless you are feeding a regular supply of fresh vegetables, a portion of commercially prepared vegetable matter should be fed to your cichlids daily.

Serve a prepared food that is suitable for the age and species of your fish, according to whether the food sinks or floats and is large or small, delicate or firm. This will take a little research, coupled with a bit of trial and error, until you discern exactly which of these foods matches the eating capabilities of your cichlids.

Commercially prepared foods absorb a good deal of moisture,

Cichlids

Prepared foods come in several forms for different types of feeders, including sticks and wafers of various sizes.

Food For Thought

so be certain to keep in mind the expansion that will occur once they have entered the aquarium water, and once they have been consumed. Also, make sure the food does not end up sitting in the substrate, expanding and polluting your tank. Remember, do not overfeed!

Take note of the expiration date on the container of your prepared foods when you buy them. Keep in mind that once opened and exposed to the air, the vitamins and nutrients will begin to lose their potency. Many aquarists pour out a small amount for use into a separate container, and then store the rest of the food in the freezer until needed.

Live Foods

There is nothing as good as live food to enhance the diet of your cichlids! Plant and animal matter of all sizes billow in clouds throughout natural waterways and, along with insects that land on the water's surface, hatching larvae, and worms that edge through the muddy banks, make up much of what cichlids consume. All of the flakes, pellets, and wafers may be state-of-the-art in their content, variety, and palatability,

Most cichlids will eat any kind of food you offer, but living foods always will be the most well received!

Know Before You Go

Before you ever collect anything from the wild, check local laws and regulations about doing so. It is often against the law to collect fish and other creatures from the wild, so make sure in advance that you're not planning anything illegal or harmful to the environment.

but there is nothing like a squirmy, wormy, squiggly, living insect to create a spirited chaos among your aquarium residents! It surely won't be long before they're quivering and strutting, courting each other, and, at times, even beckoning to you!

The mental and emotional value, in and of itself, is reason enough to make live foods worthwhile. As we know with humans and our other pets, an upbeat state of mind works wonders on one's overall health and well-being. A happy mind, a healthy body!

Live foods have also been found to provide those minute, or trace, vitamins and minerals, some of which science still cannot replicate in prepared foods

properly enough for our cichlids. The addition of just one missing ingredient in the diet can really improve the health of your cichlids.

What to Look For

The variety of live foods is boundless, and in nature there are seasonal times for most of this fare. You might enjoy going outside with your boots on, a net and bucket in tow, to collect your bounty while it is lush. As you do so, to assure the pureness of your catch be certain that you are far off the path of traffic and pollutants.

Our own home propagations may be regulated by the seasons, but we do have a bit more leeway than nature in that we have the ability to culture many of the foods indoors throughout the year. You can start with some infusorians—tiny organisms that live in green pond water and that fry love to eat—by keeping them in a warm container with some lettuce.

Brine Shrimp

Baby brine shrimp are a very popular and nutritious food for fry and small cichlids, with even medium-size cichlids becoming quite emotionally inspired by their presence. Baby brine shrimp are excellent for bringing your cichlids into spawning condition and widely used by successful aquarists.

Adult brine shrimp provide superb roughage and, given the work involved in culturing them, are best purchased at your local aquarium store. Adult brine shrimp alone are not in any manner an adequate diet.

Worms

Various types of worms make good eats for your cichlids. Microworms are particularly beneficial for fry and small cichlids that hover and pick along the bottom of the tank. Grindal worms and white worms, both much larger than microworms, are relished. They sink to the bottom, where they will remain alive for several hours or longer if left uneaten. As with all excess foods, be certain to remove the uneaten portions shortly after the initial feeding.

Earthworms are an excellent source of protein and vitamins, are an exceptionally clean food, and are easy to culture. They may be fed whole or cut, depending on the size of the mouths of your cichlids. Earthworms will sink to the bottom, but when fed to medium and large fish they rarely make it past the eagerly gaping jaws! Earthworms must be fed in moderation due to their

high protein content, and once again, are not to be considered as a food source for *Tropheus* and other herbivorous cichlids.

Blackworms are a rich and excellent food as long as they are rinsed under extremely cold water once a day, and kept cold and fresh. Also not to be considered as a food source for *Tropheus* and other herbivorous cichlids, blackworms must be purchased from a reliable source, and you need to be aware that by feeding blackworms you risk introducing pathogens into your tank. However, the benefits in this case do outweigh the potential risks when the product is stored and cared for properly. Because of the difficulty of getting them from unpolluted sources, tubifex worms are not recommended.

If you're raising worms or other live foods, you might want to add yeast or other vitamin-enriched prepared foods to what you feed them,

Small and Squiggly

Starter cultures of worms and other live foods that are easy to propagate at home are only occasionally available at pet shops, but you can obtain them by mail from advertisers in the classified sections of aquarium magazines like *Tropical Fish Hobbyist*. The starter cultures normally come with full instructions for setting up and feeding the animals and harvesting the crop.

since these additives will ultimately end up being ingested by, and therefore benefiting, your cichlids. Both Grindal worms and white worms have a high fat content and should be fed sparingly, though. Neither is suitable for *Tropheus* and other long-intestined herbivorous cichlids.

Daphnia

Aquatic crustaceans of the genus *Daphnia* and related genera are an excellent food when fed as a supplement, mentally stimulating the predatory instincts of your small- to medium-size cichlids (these "water fleas" swim throughout the tank). As they are filter feeders, *Daphnia* are rich in vitamins and algal matter, and their shells provide excellent roughage. *Daphnia* are enjoyable to cultivate outside in a small pool, tub, or pond.

Mosquito Larvae

These are a wonderful food that is relished by almost all cichlids. But remember, if left uneaten they will develop into mosquitoes!

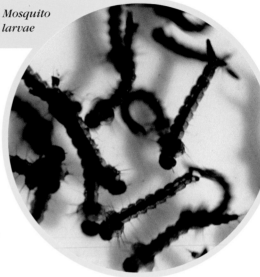

Mosquito larvae

Feeder Fish

With so many other excellent alternatives, feeder goldfish, which are raised specifically as food for other animals, are not recommended, unless you want to raise them in your own controlled, disease-free tanks. Even in this case, there is no reason to risk creating such an explosion of pollutants caused by the excessive waste at feeding time.

Other Fresh, Meaty Foods

There are alternatives to live foods that will not have the added appeal of movement, but will be certain to spark interest, particularly among

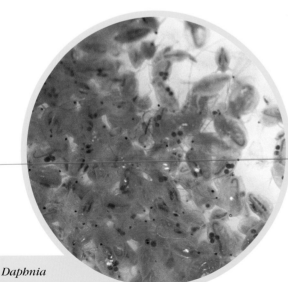

Daphnia

your medium to large omnivorous and carnivorous cichlids. Fresh white fish such as cod, tilefish, or striped bass, as well as salmon, clams, scallops, shrimp, and lobster will all be relished when minced with a knife or blended in a food processor. Make sure that the foods thus processed not be reduced to a particle size too fine to be eaten readily.

Frozen Foods

Many foods are now available in a frozen state and are widely used by aquarists. These include brine shrimp, bloodworms, beef heart, krill, glassworms, and various blended preparations.

Bloodworms, the larvae of a midge, are a prevalent food source in many freshwater habitats; and are quite valuable for conditioning your

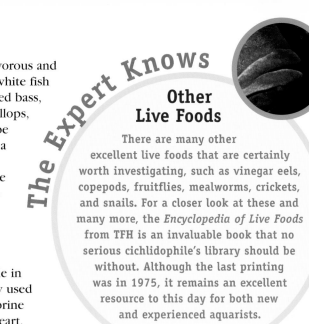

cichlids for spawning. They are most conveniently sold in a frozen state and come in the form of individual cubes or flat packs from which pieces can be broken off. Some aquarists choose to feed frozen foods by throwing an entire cube into the tank straight from the freezer. Alternatively, defrosting frozen bloodworms, brine shrimp, and krill in a small strainer and then rinsing them with cold water will assist greatly in removing pollutant-causing excess moisture and scum.

As for frozen foods in general, the amount of vitamins and nutrients retained in a useable state through the freezing process

Your cichlids will relish frozen bloodworms as part of their diet.

most diets in nature, whether the fish is herbivorous or ominivorous. Some cichlids actually eat only plant matter. Many of the prepared foods, as mentioned previously, will take care of the vegetable requirements of your fishes. However, none is as good as a large leaf of romaine lettuce placed into the tank, which you will most certainly know if you have ever witnessed the delightful glee of a group of large *Uaru*, with their bright orange eyes flashing at the sight of this delicacy! Providing fresh greenery is a wonderful way to supply vegetable matter, as it satisfies the necessary nutritional needs of many of your cichlids and provides them with interest and activity throughout the day.

There are many excellent options here, such as cut green beans or pieces of zucchini that have been blanched lightly, and dark green leaves such as spinach or the aforementioned lettuce. Unsalted canned peas are relished by many cichlids. Start by trying out a few at a time and, once they become accustomed to the delicious flavor, feed to your eager eaters in moderation, since peas are quite rich in carbohydrates. Take a look through your refrigerator, be creative, and have fun!

is perpetually a topic of debate among aquarists. Frozen foods are a favorite of many, but be certain to feed with attentive care.

Freeze-Dried Foods

Freeze drying retains much of the original nutrition and taste appeal, but in a much more convenient form. Many food organisms are available, including brine shrimp, krill, daphnia, cyclops, bloodworms, and more. You can toss a piece into the tank and let the feeding frenzy begin, or you can press the food against the inside of the tank glass, where it will stick, providing you a close-up view of the feeding frenzy. Freeze-dried foods can also be crumbled or pulverized to feed fry.

Vegetables

Performing an essential role in the health of your cichlids, vegetable matter makes up a percentage of

Oh, the Possibilities!

There are obviously numerous variables and options to consider when contemplating the nutritional needs of our cichlids. With so many choices and alternatives, feeding a good diet is an exciting project for both you and your fishes, one that proves particularly rewarding when you successfully discover the equation that produces a tank of healthy and vibrant cichlids.

Water

Making sure all metabolic processes occur in intricate harmony within the bodies of your cichlids relies on the water in which they live. Water quality can be the determining factor in whether your fish merely get by and survive or flourish and thrive. Essential trace minerals, necessary for the health of your cichlids, are furnished by the water in which they live. As these minerals are utilized by your cichlids, the supply within the water becomes depleted. A filter can perform many

useful tasks, but it will not replace expended minerals. The most efficient manner of replenishing these trace minerals is (you guessed it!) through your routine water changes.

Variables, Choices, and Alternatives

When deliberating on the feeding regimen that best suits your cichlids, research and take into account feeding specializations within the species that you are caring for. There are omnivores, which eat an assortment of vegetables and meats; herbivores, which eat entirely, or almost entirely, vegetable matter; and carnivores, which eat primarily meat. Many of these cichlids are able to adapt to our home feeding practices, but they must do so around their characteristic physical make-up, such as jaw structure, stomach size and structure, intestinal length, and overall body shape.

Chapter 6

Prevention is the

Best
Medicine

Cichlids are hardy fishes, having evolved over millions of years, surviving through adaptation to a broad range of aquatic environments. As long as you practice the four keys to success that we have discussed throughout these pages, your cichlids, with but a few exceptions, should remain in vigorous health. It is far easier to maintain a healthy cichlid than to bring an ill fish back to good health. An ounce of prevention is definitely worth a pound of cure!

How to Know Your Fish are All Right

Get into the habit of taking a few minutes each day to take a close look at your cichlid aquarium. Check to see that the fishes are actively swimming around the tank with obvious vitality. They are probably dancing about, pressing their faces up against the glass in hopes of winning your heart—and a tasty treat! Unless they are focusing on you for a meal, your cichlids should be poking inquisitively through the aquarium substrate, foraging through the plants, around the driftwood and rocks, and into the pockets of the sponge filters, or sparring with one another. Check their eyes to see that they are bright and alert, and check their scales and body for a glimmering shine with no open wounds or blemishes. As they grow older, consider whether they have been pairing off, spawning, and caring for and raising their fry in a distinctive, nurturing fashion. If this is true, you are doing an excellent job of caring for your cichlids!

On the other hand, when you take a close look at your cichlids, do you note a lack of interest, fishes that seem to be hanging back in the dark corners and crevices? Do they seem frightened, or are they lethargic, revealing irregular, dull scales? Have they lost their appetite, or do they dart at food without taking it in, only to back off into the aquarium's shadows? Check their bodies and see whether you note any unusual tiny white spots or open abrasions.

Since some cichlids are much more active than others, it is important to observe your fish and know what thier normal behavior is so that you can detect when they are acting sick.

Hiding away is not itself a sign of stress. Here a pair of Steatocranus *peer out the front door of their nest hole.*

Are your cichlids looking all right but showing no interest in interaction with their tankmates? If you notice any of these symptoms, the first thing to do is a water change! Once you have put your siphon away, we will rejoin here and take a look at how best to provide the optimum health and care for your cichlids.

Stressed Out!

Stress, which can be brought on by many things, is the number one root of illness in cichlids. When a fish undergoes stress, such as a breakdown in water conditions, its immune system is compromised and it becomes susceptible to many illnesses. Just as when you are under stress and unrested you have a much greater chance of catching a cold or the flu, a cichlid's body suffers the same consequences. If your cichlids are not in optimal health, there is a good chance that they are being exposed to stress in one form or another.

Run Down the Stress Checklist

Have you been diligent about practicing the four keys to success with cichlids? The water that your cichlids live in can be a major cause of stress. Have you performed regular water changes? Overfeeding your cichlids breaks down the water quality, placing your cichlids under stress. Have you been overfeeding your cichlids? Are you feeding the proper foods for the species? Overcrowding your cichlids can cause a breakdown in water quality, also placing major stress on harassed inhabitants that are overwhelmed in such small quarters packed with aggression. Are your cichlids overcrowded? Your good bacteria must flourish in abundance in order to keep up with the ammonia and nitrites. The chances are that if your fishes are stressed due to water quality, your biofilter bacteria are undergoing stress as well. Are you caring for your good bacteria as you are your cichlids?

Other Stress Factors

If your cichlids still are not at their best, think of what else might be causing them stress, and before reaching for any medicine, remove the stress! Is the tank large enough for the species that you are keeping? A tank that is too small for a species, whether in physical size or design, is a major cause of stress among cichilds. Are there ample places in the aquarium for each cichlid to hide, or are one or two cichlids left exposed, with no shelter to flee to, and under the constant harassment of more antagonistic individuals?

Your Cichlid's Bogus Journey

When you buy a new fish, in many cases it has been through the stress of capture in some far-off land, then held on a small boat in a bucket, transferred onto another boat in another bucket, held there for several days, transported to a holding facility and dumped into a large vat with hundreds of other cichlids, packed in a foam box, trucked over a bumpy, pothole-filled dirt road for miles, stuck into a cargo bay, loaded onto an airplane, shipped to another airport, held in another cargo bay, loaded onto another plane, shipped many miles overseas, made to linger in another airport, loaded onto a truck, unloaded again, and finally placed into a little tank that certainly bears no resemblance to where it lived before that big frightful net wrapped around it. And that was just to get to the pet store; it now has to travel to your home, too!

Constant fear is a major cause of stress among cichlids—and wouldn't you be stressed too?

Is the water too hot or too cold? Is the tank placed below waist level in an area where people are constantly rushing by? Are there catfish or other inhabitants in the tank that appear innocent enough but are up to no good when your back is turned? Are your cichlids getting enough dark, quiet hours at night in which to sleep? Have you recently added a new piece of wood or decor to the tank that might be leaching a harmful substance into the water? If something is in question, take it out, do a water change, wait a day or two, and see if that clears up the problem.

The Quarantine Tank

Consider this all-too-common scenario. You proudly have your cichlid aquarium established, and all the inhabitants are healthy and vibrant, maybe even spawning for you. Upon entering an aquarium shop, another cichlid just knocks you over, it is to-die-for gorgeous! It would look great in your tank and you just have to have it. Home it comes and after adjusting it to your water, in it goes with your other cichlids, and after making it through the initial gauntlet of attacks by the other cichlids, things seem to settle down nicely. But the next morning, all your original cichlids are hanging listlessly, their fins are clamped tight, slime is peeling away from their sides, and their breathing is labored. You do a water change, but they do not revive; the next day they are all dead. The only fish left delightedly cavorting about the tank is the new cichlid that you just added.

Sound farfetched? Sadly, it happens all the time to countless hobbyists, but hopefully it happens only once! Fish can be carriers of disease and not show outward signs of disease themselves. Or they may have undergone extreme stress and their immune system is beginning to break down, causing an as-yet-undetected pathogenic disease to take hold.

Using a quarantine tank can prevent a disastrous spread of disease and is an essential part of your success in keeping cichlids. Placing each new fish into a small, quiet tank where it can become adjusted and any illness that it might harbor will have a chance to show itself and be treated is a critical step to take before introducing it into your established cichlid aquarium. A 10-gallon (38-l) tank is perfect for most cichlids; set it in an area that does not receive traffic. The objectives when setting up the quarantine tank are to make it as comfortable and stress free as possible for the newcomer(s). Paint the outside of the bottom and back of the tank with a dark, non-glossy paint, leave a bare bottom with no gravel, place no light on the top, and place several PVC

Quarantine tanks needn't be all that glamorous, they just need to be clean and large enough to accommodate whatever fish you put in them.

No Babies Here

The quarantine tank can also be used as a hospital tank if you have an injured cichlid or one that requires medication. But it is not a good idea to use this tank for raising fry. You'll need yet another tank for those little guys.

pipes or one or two ceramic tunnels in sizes appropriate for the species. Place a heater set at 80°F into the tank, put a thermometer strip on the outside, and hook up one or two bacteria-filled sponge filters. Do not add excess substrate or intricate decorations that cannot easily be cleaned and rid of pathogens.

Any new fish must be placed into this tank for a minimum of three weeks, though preferably four to six weeks. This gives ample time to spot and treat any disease and allows the fish time to calm down after the stress of a long ordeal.

A separate siphon and bucket must be used to change the water in the quarantine tank, and water changes are a major part of the regimen of care. Other than that, feed the fish well and let it remain quiet and undisturbed. Be certain to wash your

hands thoroughly with an antibacterial soap after working with this tank; then, for the sake of all your fishes, rinse your hands really well to be certain that there is no soap left on them! It is best to do any chores with the quarantine tank last.

Common Cichlid Ailments

As we have discussed, with proper preventative care, cichlids do not become ill easily or often. But there are a few ailments that you need to be aware of. If you spot any symptoms of any kind, consult with your veterinarian before even considering any treatment other than quarantining.

Injuries

Rowdy characters that they are, cichlids tend to receive anything from torn fins to large open wounds from their unruly cohorts. Usually these wounds will heal with time—fins will grow back, scales will repair, and minor abrasions will mend. The main consideration is to keep the water clean. The mucous secretion on a cichlid's body contains natural antibodies that ward off both parasites and bacterial infection. When this mucus is blemished, even by the

More Info

For an in-depth look into illnesses, check the Resources section at the back of this book. Many of the materials and organizations can share information on the subject.

fabric of a fish net, the potency of the immune system decreases and the risk of infection increases. When the water quality is poor, significant environmental stress compounds the issue, placing undue strain on the skin's natural defenses, and bacterial infection can occur. Therefore if an injury does occur, do an immediate water change, and continue to do so each day until you see significant improvement.

If, after your efforts, a fungal infection takes hold, transfer the injured fish to the hospital tank. Add one to two tablespoons of non-iodized aquarium salt per gallon to the water and set the temperature at 82°F (28°C). In this case, an antifungal medication may be necessary.

Consult with your veterinarian about which medicine to use, follow the instructions carefully for the recommended duration, and do not add another medicine.

Ich

At one time or another most aquarists will come across *Ichthyophthirius multifiliis*, commonly known as ich or ick. This is a parasite that digs under the skin of the fish, feeding off its flesh and creating numerous small white dots that cover the body. Extremely contagious as well as lethal, ich can be eradicated when treated immediately and the fish will be fine. When you detect ich on one fish, you must treat all the tank's inhabitants.

Cichlids are rowdy and likely to injure the weak fish in your tank, which can lead to some ugly infections.

A fish infected with ich looks like it's been dusted with table salt.

Ich is not salt or heat tolerant, so add two tablespoons of aquarium salt per gallon (4 L) and raise the heat to 88°F (31°C). The higher heat will cause a lower level of dissolved oxygen, though, so be certain that there is ample aeration and, as always when treating them, observe your fishes for signs of stress. Excellent medications are made specifically for treating ich. Follow the instructions on the label carefully and continue for the recommended duration.

HITH Disease

Hole in the head disease, or head and lateral line erosion, is common among large cichlids that are overfed, kept in crowded quarters, or not treated to sufficient water changes. The sensory pores that we discussed in Chapter 2 become pitted, mostly around the head region, and if left long enough can eventually lead to massive head erosion. Fixing these three causes, especially including a strict regimen of large water changes, often reverses the pitting.

Good to Know

The Bare Medicine Cabinet

A concoction of medicines thrown into the tank by a well-intentioned aquarist can result in far greater damage and has caused more deaths among fishes than has actual illness. Preventative medicines are by far the best and do not take up much room in your medicine cabinet (but nevertheless should be used sparingly). The items that you may wish to keep are salt and an anti-ich medication. Just remember, for the millionth time, there is no greater tonic than a water change coupled with common sense.

Keeping your cichlids healthy is primarily a matter of proper maintenance and husbandry.

Chapter 7

So Many Cichlids to
Choose
From

BY David E. Boruchowitz

Cichlids are among the most successful vertebrates
in the world. There are more than 2,000 species,
and more are being discovered all the time. Cichlids
have filled almost every niche in their habitats and
are found in North, Central, and South America,
Africa, and Asia.

There are cichlids that mature at less than an inch (3 cm), and there are 3-foot-long (1-meter-long) cichlids, plus all sizes in between. You can find cichlids in soft, acidic water and in hard, basic water. There are cichlids in freshwater habitats, brackish habitats, and marine habitats. There are schooling cichlids and loners that tolerate others of their kind only for breeding. There are cichlid species in which both parents care for the young, others in which the mother takes that job, and still others in which it is the father that cares for the brood. Some cichlids tend their eggs within a defined territory, some care for them in a cave, and others carry their eggs in their mouths until they hatch. Certain cichlids are extremely peaceful and never harm other fishes, but some ornery cichlids seem always ready to pick a fight.

With all these variations, there is at least one cichlid species for everyone. Do you like them small and peaceful, or large and nasty? Small and nasty, or large and peaceful? Subtly colored or flamboyantly hued? Gregarious or sociopathic? Easy to keep and breed, or incredibly challenging? No matter what kind of fish you are looking for, there are cichlids that will fit the bill. Let's take a look at the world of cichlids and point out a few species that are particularly good ambassadors for the family, with a proven track record of turning unsuspecting aquarists into unapologetic cichlid addicts.

North America

Although there is one cichlid whose native range includes the United States—the Texas cichlid *Herichthys cyanoguttatus*—all other North American cichlids are found in

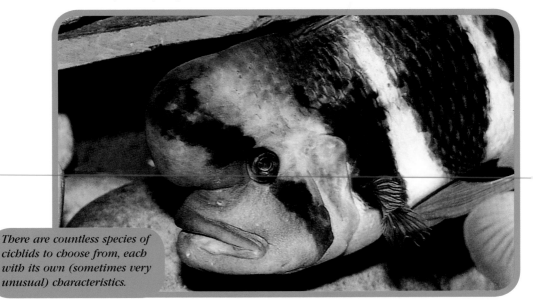

There are countless species of cichlids to choose from, each with its own (sometimes very unusual) characteristics.

Which Cichlid is Best for Me?

Cichlids can be partly divided into groups based on geography, since the species found in one region are often similar. In the following section you will meet a group of cichlids that fit these criteria:

- Commonly available
- Inexpensive (believe it or not, some cichlids can cost several hundred dollars apiece!)
- Easy to care for
- Easy to breed

These few species are merely the tip of the cichlid iceberg, but once you gain experience with them you will be ready to go on to more challenging species. That does not mean that you will necessarily never look back, for many lifelong cichlidophiles reserve a special place in their hearts—and in their fishrooms—for those personable, colorful species that first intrigued them with their beauty, personality, and parental dedication.

Mexico, Central America, and on some Caribbean islands. The water in their habitats is for the most part moderately hard and neutral to basic, but most species are quite adaptable to different water chemistries. All these fish are biparental substrate spawners, and many of them spawn in caves or crevices. While they normally pair up to spawn, occasionally a male will raise two broods simultaneously, splitting his time and energies between two females. This happens in nature as well as in captivity.

North American cichlids are all closely related, but they are highly diversified. They range in size from true dwarfs to gigantic tankbusters, and various species are adapted to eat algae, small invertebrates, terrestrial plants, or other fishes. Many wonderful aquarium candidates can be found among the cichlids of this continent!

CRYPTOHEROS NIGROFASCIATUS

The convict cichlid is a mainstay of the hobby and one of the best cichlids to start out with. Its beautiful colors, small size, feisty personality, and fierce parental care have possibly brought more people into the cichlid hobby than all other species combined.

Males do not usually exceed 4 to 5 inches (10 to 13 cm), while females are smaller. Although cichlids as a group tend to breed long before they have reached full size, convicts are particularly precocious, and females less than an inch (3 cm) long have been known to raise a spawn with inch-long males.

This species's feistiness is legendary. Parents with fry have been observed in Lake Nicaragua successfully driving off giant predatory cichlids that could have ended the attack simply by swallowing the tiny terrors.

The species shows enormous variation over a very large natural range, and domesticated strains vary greatly in coloration as well. Females sport more color, especially in an iridescent green-blue blotch on the dorsal fin and a large, iridescent orange-red patch on the belly. Two domesticated color morphs have been established—the white or pink convict, which has no dark pigmentation except for its eyes, and the marble, calico, or OB convict, which has black splotches on a pink body.

Although larger is always better, a 15- or 20-gallon (57- to 76-l) tank is adequate for a breeding pair, but it is vital that there are numerous caves in which one or the other fish can hide. It is very common for

Cryptoheros nigrofasciatus

disputes to break out, and although it is typical for the smaller female to be injured or killed, once in a while it is the male. A cave is also the favored spawning site, and the female often lays her eggs on the roof of the cave. And, as nasty as the parents can be to each other, they are the most diligent of parents, even compared to other cichlids.

HERICHTHYS CYANOGUTTATUS

Known as the Texas cichlid or Rio Grande perch, this magnificent cichlid is appropriate only for large aquariums, as it grows to about a foot (30 cm) in length. Females are much smaller than males and may breed at only 2 inches (5 cm). Think in terms of a 50- or 75-gallon (189- or 284-l) tank for a single specimen and a

Herichthys cyanoguttatus

100-gallon (379-l) or larger tank for a pair. This fish is an omnivore and must have plant matter in its diet. It will sift through the gravel for bits of food, destroying any plantings or aquascaping in the process. Make sure any rocks are placed securely so they cannot topple if undermined by the cichlid's digging. It is aggressive, but not excessively; that is, you can keep it with other fishes of similar size and temperament, as long as they have enough room and are not spawning.

The body and fins are covered with iridescent blue spangles, but when breeding the fish take on a split coloration, with the front half of the body white and the back half black.

Thorichthys meeki

THORICHTHYS MEEKI
Known as the firemouth cichlid, this beautiful fish has a red throat. When it wishes to appear threatening, it flares its gill covers, exposing its entire crimson throat. An "eyespot" on each gill cover completes the menacing image. Males get to be about 6 to 7 inches (15 to 18 cm), and while females are generally smaller, there isn't usually as great a size difference between the sexes as there is in, say, convicts. These are fairly peaceful fish; in fact, in a mixed cichlid community, they may be bullied by smaller species. A pair should have at least a 30-gallon (114-l) tank with numerous caves. While not quite as easy to breed as convicts, firemouths will raise a brood for you if they are well

conditioned and if you maintain water quality with frequent large water changes.

In nature this fish gets most of its food by sifting sand, using its mouth as a shovel to scoop up a mouthful of substrate, which it expels through its gills. Algae, small invertebrates, and other food objects are trapped in the gill rakers and then swallowed. Although firemouths will take all standard aquarium fare, you will still see this behavior if their tank has a fine gravel or sand bottom.

South America
South American cichlids are extremely diverse and belong to many different groups, so it is impossible to generalize very much about them. There are many species that come from rainforest waters, which are extremely soft and acidic, and some need that type of

So Many Cichlids to Choose From

water for successful spawning. Many others are much more adaptable, and two very popular South American cichlids should do well for you no matter what your water supply is like.

Port Cichlids

Although port cichlds are often labeled *Cichlasoma portalegrense*, there are actually several similar species imported under that name. Fortunately, they all need the same type of care. They are chunky, medium-size cichlids, usually about 5 to 6 inches (13 to 15 cm), with males slightly larger. These fish have a subtle beauty, having a somber gray background accentuated by a dark reticulation around the scales. Highlights of iridescent color catch the light as the fish moves, and several species have breeding coloration that

includes color such as a red tail fin. These cichlids are biparental substrate spawners, but they usually choose a flat surface out in the open, not in a cave, as the spawning site. A 30-gallon (114-l) tank is adequate for a pair of

*"Aequidens"
pulcher*

these fish, and they are sufficiently mild mannered that they can often be kept with other types of fishes such as large barbs or livebearers.

"AEQUIDENS" PULCHER
Known as the blue acara, this cichlid is about the same size and shape as the port cichlids, but individuals are marked with iridescent blue squiggles on their faces and iridescent blue spangles on their bodies. Males are larger and more colorful. They are biparental spawners who usually choose a flat rock as a spawning site.

African Rift Lakes
The last four decades of the twentieth century saw a cichlid craze caused by the introduction of cichlids from the great lakes of Africa. Hundreds upon hundreds of species of cichlids were discovered, many of them drop-dead gorgeous and all of them fascinating. The lakes they come from have high concentrations of dissolved minerals, and these cichlids are happiest in hard, basic water.

A Little Bit Different
A great many species, including all cichlids endemic to lakes Malawi and Victoria, are mouthbrooders, usually maternal. But the two selected for inclusion here are substrate spawners.

Julidochromis ornatus

JULIDOCHROMIS ORNATUS
Sometimes called a dwarf *Julidochromis*, this perky yellow-and-black cichlid grows to only a little over 3 inches (8 cm) long. It is torpedo shaped and lives naturally in rock piles in Lake Tanganyika. One of its endearing habits is its movement in and around the rocks—it almost always keeps its belly oriented to the nearest rock, which means that as it moves over the rock, always alert for the tiny organisms that make up its diet, it will go from right side up to upside down, always keeping its belly next to the rock surface.

Although these fish breed in pairs, placing their eggs in a well-defended crevice or cavity among the rocks, they do not defend their young as most cichlids do. Instead, they defend their territory. In the dynamics of their natural home in the lake, it is vital for them to remain within their small territory, from which they chase all intruders. If one of their fry strays outside the territory, they do not leave to fetch it back. It is fascinating to place some food into the tank and then watch the fry swarm out of their cave to snap up whatever drifts into their territory, then zip back into the safety of the rocks like so many tiny little bees.

Like almost all other Rift Lake cichlids, these little fish are extremely aggressive. They will not bother fishes outside their small territories, which tend to be roughly spherical around their home cave, but absolutely any other fish will be forcibly driven from the area. In a 4-foot (122-cm) tank, like a 75- or 90-gallon (284- or 341-l), you could keep two pairs. With a rock pile at each end of the tank, they will divide the

The Expert Knows

Family Ties

With *Julidochromis ornatus*, the older offspring may assist in the protection of their younger siblings, with the entire family defending the breeding territory! Also, it is common to have fry of various sizes coexisting with their parents in a breeding tank, which is not too common with many other cichlids. Often, despite their strong parenting skills, other cichlids will start to eat some of the young fry as they grow a little older.

space, with each pair keeping to its half. A 20-gallon (76-l) tank or larger is adequate for a single breeding pair and their fry.

LAMPROLOGUS OCELLATUS
These Tanganyikan cichlids are shelldwellers. They live in empty snail shells—or, in captivity, in substitute "shells" like PVC elbows. There should be several more shells than fish to minimize fights over the "best" ones. These fish grow to about 2 inches (5 cm) in length, so they fit nicely in a large snail shell. Their gold and blue iridescence and spunky bulldog personality make them a perennial favorite.

In the wild they are harem spawners, with a male holding a territory in which several females' shells are located.

Lamprologus ocellatus

You can imitate this, but the fish will also spawn as pairs if kept that way. A 10-gallon (38-l) tank is large enough for a pair. The female cares for the eggs and fry inside her shell, while the male protects the territory. In a harem, each female defends her own mini-territory within the male's—mainly from the other females.

Because these fish have such tiny territories, they can be kept in large community tanks. A 6-foot (2-m) tank with a cluster of shells on the substrate can house a great variety of fishes, plus the shelldwellers, who will stay very close to their shells. The only exception is if there are two males in the tank; in that case, even a 6-foot (2-m) tank can be too small, as the dominant male will attack the other mercilessly, chasing him all over the aquarium. It is fascinating to watch the dynamics of a group of these fish as they tend their shells and posture to each other.

Other Africans

Before the Rift Lake cichlid craze, Africa supplied the hobby with many interesting cichlids, and they are still popular. The following are almost

always available, including in some domestic color varieties.

PELVICACHROMIS PULCHER

Known as the krib (from an older scientific name, *kribensis*), this species should be the poster child for community cichlids. Not only does it coexist with other fishes peacefully and leave plants alone, it will often raise a brood in a community tank—without losing the fry and without decimating its tankmates. Both sexes are beautiful, but the smaller, plumper female's breeding coloration includes a red-violet belly. The male will reach about 4 inches (10 cm).

A favorite spawning site is an inverted clay

Pelvicachromis pulcher

Hemichromis lifalili

Rift Lake cichlids were known. They can, however, definitely take care of themselves, and it is important to watch a courting pair carefully in case things get violent. It is best, as always, to let the fish pair up naturally in a group. A 30-gallon (114-ls) or larger aquarium will work for a breeding pair.

Madagascar and Asia

The cichlids of Madagascar and Asia are among the most primitive, resembling the original ancestors of all cichlids. Malagasy cichlids are either extinct or endangered, and they are not easy to keep, so they should be kept only by experienced aquarists in species preservation programs. There are three Asian species of cichlids in the genus *Etroplus*, one of which has been a staple of the hobby for decades.

ETROPLUS MACULATUS

Known as the chromide, the yellow chromide, the orange chromide, and the red chromide, this species has maintained a constant presence in the hobby even though it has never been extremely popular. The domestic red strain is probably the easiest to find. These fish reach about 3 inches (8 cm), and sexes can be difficult to distinguish. The wild type is a yellowish fish with dark markings, while the red variety lacks all the dark coloration.

This cichlid is a little harder to breed than most of the others listed here, but a well-conditioned pair should spawn as long as water quality is maintained. They do best and are most likely to

flowerpot with a notch broken into the rim, creating a doorway into the pot. Although the krib will spawn in a wide range of water chemistries, the pH—the relative acidity or basicity of the water—will affect the sex ratio of the youngsters.

HEMICHROMIS LIFALILI

The original jewel cichlid in the hobby was identified as *Hemichromis bimaculatus*, but there are actually several species sporting bright red color with iridescent blue spangles that may have been imported. In recent years, fish identified as *H. lifalili* have become very popular due to their smaller size (about 3¼ inches, or 8 cm, for males) and the fact that they have more red coloration outside of breeding.

Everything is relative—jewels used to have a reputation as being nasty, but that was before the really aggressive

breed when fed plenty of vegetable-based foods and kept in slightly brackish water.

Pterophyllum scalare

Two Special Species

There are two species of cichlids that are so popular that many beginners wind up with them in their aquariums. The fact that neither is a very good choice for a first aquarium, which is likely to be a community tank, does not seem to lessen their appeal! Because they are so appealing, you may very well be tempted to try one or both. Even though a beginner's community tank isn't the right place for them, it is not difficult to provide these fish with the proper conditions. Let's discuss them briefly so you can make an informed decision.

Angelfish–*PTEROPHYLLUM SCALARE*

Many people are surprised to find out that angelfish are cichlids, and not just because of their unusual shape. Angels are extremely peaceful for a large

cichlid, and not usually territorial except when breeding. They will, however, hunt down any fish small enough to be swallowed, and they have long, trailing fins. Both these traits make them bad choices for community tanks, where they will eat the neon tetras and be picked on by

Etroplus maculatus

Angelfish have been bred in many color varieties, but they're all peaceful, pretty fishes.

tiger barbs, who cannot resist those delicate fins!

Angels have been bred in a variety of strains. Most of the established mutations are in color, but there are also extra-long finnage and pearled scales. One of the hottest varieties currently is called the koi angel, and it is a combination of the gold marble and blushing traits. Originally with orange on the top of the head, koi angels have been selectively bred to the point that there are all-orange specimens. Practiced aquarists can reliably determine the sex of angelfish by appearance, but the differences are subtle and best

learned from someone who can point them out on actual specimens.

The best way to keep angels is with other species big enough not to become snacks and peaceful enough to live and let live. An all-angel community makes a spectacular display, and it is the best way to get breeding pairs, since the fish can choose their own mates. A pair of angels will select a vertical or slanted surface—a leaf, the side of the aquarium, or a piece of slate standing in their tank—as a spawning site. Many people find that their angelfish pairs will eat their eggs or their fry, but others prove dutiful parents.

Oscars—*Astronotus ocellatus*

Oscars appeal to everyone. Their outgoing personalities and puppy-dog faces are enough to win people over, and a single specimen often becomes a true pet, interacting with its keeper through the glass. Unfortunately, a common scenario is for an unsuspecting aquarist to purchase a baby oscar and bring it home to a community tank. In a short time the oscar has grown large enough to eat all its tankmates, and it continues to grow until it dies from the pollution in its too-small aquarium.

This tragedy can be prevented, and anyone who wishes to invest the time and money can enjoy having a pet oscar that will greet its owner and excitedly beg for a treat. Just how big a tank does an oscar need? That depends on a lot of factors, but a good rule of thumb is to allow 25 to 50 gallons (95 to 189 l) per oscar. Oscars over a foot (30 cm) long are not uncommon. They have thick bodies and are voracious, extremely messy eaters of meaty foods. Big tanks, super filtration, and massive water changes are the way to keep an oscar happy and healthy. They are particularly sensitive to poor water quality and will often develop head and lateral line erosion if water changes are skimped on.

The only way to tell the sex of an oscar is to examine its genital opening, but oscars are notoriously fussy about choosing a mate, so not knowing an oscar's sex doesn't really matter much, as placing a male and female together rarely works. Raising a group together is the best way to get a pair, as they have no trouble telling each other apart. Obviously a large aquarium is needed to grow a group to maturity, and then a large tank is needed for the spawning pair, since they can easily produce 1,000 or more offspring in one clutch. They make ferocious parents, and it is indeed an amazing sight to see such massive fish gingerly caring for their tiny newly hatched fry.

Oscars come in many color varieties but all of them have personality galore.

Chapter 8

Breeding Cichlids and
Beyond

So far we have focused on choosing and maintaining your cichlids. One of the most fascinating and greatest joys of keeping cichlids is their engaging parental care. Tending of the eggs and the fry may be handled by one or both parents, each fulfilling its own separate role in the process. Through an understanding of our cichlids, the challenge for us as aquarists is to work with their inherent needs as defined by nature, allowing them the optimal environment to breed and raise their young within the confines of the five walls of our aquariums.

ou should empathize with the complexities of your cichlids' mission to raise their young to adulthood. It is not an easy task for them to begin with, and it is only made more difficult by the five walls of your aquarium and any other inhabitants living within the inescapable confines of their territory.

Parental Behavior

The diverse and intriguing parental behavior of cichlids is one their most alluring qualities, and there are as many variations in parental behavior as there are species of cichlids, which adds to the fascination and the desire to add that one more tank and keep that one more species. Some cichlids breed in monogamous pairs and others are polygamous.

Monogamous Cichlids

In the case of monogamous cichlids, a pair bond is formed, according to celebrated ichthyologist Dr. Paul Loiselle, "for a single reproductive episode," and when the gonadal cycles of the male and female are in synch. The hostility that the male and female cichlid may express toward each other is

turned toward outside intruders once a spawning site has been established.

Therefore, when setting up the cichlid aquarium with the intent of having your fish breed, keep in mind the choices and natural forces your fish would undergo were they to be in the wild. In general we tend to deal with our monogamous cichlids in an anthropomorphic manner, as if they had been officially wed and are to live happily ever after as a couple. In nature, pair bonding is formed by the monogamous duo with the intent of reproducing as many offspring as quickly and efficiently as possible within that

The Expert Knows

Reproduction is Hard Work

An important factor to keep in mind is that whatever your breeding cichlids' actions may be, each is meant to ensure that the species will continue to survive into the future. Precious energy is rationed and focused on making certain that those eggs hatch and that those young are offered the best opportunity possible to grow into adults and to one day raise their own young in turn. Energy is not a commodity to be taken lightly or expended unnecessarily. Therefore the parents will be extremely territorial during the period of breeding and parenting. They will kill another cichlid or other fish if that is what it takes to ensure the survival of those young. Will they go out of their way to kill another cichlid that is not in their territory? No, because that would expend energy that they cannot afford to waste.

Discus take the normal cichlid parenting duties one step further and feed their fry with secretions from their bodies. You can see several of the babies grazing on each parent.

particular reproductive cycle. There will be no hesitation the moment one of the partners sees clear to dash out of the match and head on to other reproductive opportunities, leaving mom or dad with the kids!

If we intend for a monogamous pair to reproduce once and then turn around and reproduce again, we now see that this would be quite out of character for these two fish in their natural environment. We need to present reasons for them to be sexually driven together to breed again. Otherwise, if left to the confines of the walls of the aquarium with no place to flee, the end result may be for one to drive the other

away with an extreme aggression and eventually kill it.

Excellent reasons for a pair bond to form or to increase the possibility of multiple spawns are the defense of a feeding territory and the defense of a spawning site. In the wild, other fishes of the same and different species will occupy the area, forcing the pair of cichlids to defend their territory. You can emulate this in the aquarium by adding other suitable fish, termed as "target" fishes, which will trigger an initial defense for food and later develop into a defense of the chosen spawning territory.

Nothing brings together a pair of would-be lovefish like the mutual need to fight off marauding invaders to protect their territory.

Polygamous Cichlids

The courtship and breeding of polygamous cichlids are quite different from those of monogamous cichlids. Polygamous cichlids are divided into two groups: that of harem polygamy and that of open polygamy.

In the case of harem polygamy, one male stakes out his territory, defending it fiercely against all other male intruders. His vast province is made up of numerous spawning sites, each held by a female. The male makes his regular rounds among the ladies, spawning with each as they become sexually ready to accept his advances. Once the spawning is complete, the female makes it clear that she wants nothing more to do with the male, swiftly and effectively evicting him from her territory. The female proceeds with her sole maternal care of the eggs and eventual fry. The male is finished with his parental duties here and swims off in search of another willing partner, although in some cases he returns to help defend the young.

Open polygamous spawners may spawn with several different partners within one sexual reproductive cycle, with no regard for the structure of a harem. All open polygamous spawners are maternal mouthbrooders—the female picks her eggs up in her mouth immediately after depositing them, at which point the male fertilizes them. In many cases the male sports spots known as "egg dummies" on his anal fin, or in some cases at the tips of long, trailing ventral fins. These spots resemble an egg, attracting the female and encouraging her to pick them up along with her

Room to Move

Cichlids that practice harem polygamy require a sizable space in a home aquarium, as there must be ample real estate to support a defensible territory for each female. If the male enters any of these territories after the spawning, he will be persecuted and ousted by the female. Therefore the male must be given a place of refuge from the severe attacks of his previous consorts.

mouthful of eggs. Her nipping at these false eggs alerts the male to fertilize the real eggs. The female may repeat this process with several other males until she is satisfied that all her eggs are fertilized. She then retreats to a protected area to avoid harassment and brood her eggs for up to several weeks before releasing the hatched fry. The males take on no parental responsibilities and are free to spread their wealth of fertility among as many females as they are clever and dashing enough to attract.

Just as with harem polygamous spawners, a home aquarium needs to provide abundant space when housing open polygamous spawners. These cichlids must be kept in groups to disperse the aggression, and although it is best to maintain single-species tanks, more than one species can be housed together as long as they are dissimilar in appearance. If only one species is maintained, a single male to several females is preferable.

The Ingredients for a Successful Spawning

The most essential ingredients in having a successful spawning are a male and a female (naturally). This may seem elementary, but it is not always that easy, as many cichlids are isomorphic, meaning that the males and the females

within a species look identical. As cichlids are not particularly fond of new introductions into their social circles once matured, the best method of procuring a male and a female is to place a group of at least five or six young specimens of your chosen species into one tank and let them grow up together. Chances are great that you will have at least one male and one female within the group.

As your fish reach maturity, a male and female likely will pair off and begin their courtship ritual. At this point you must observe the relationship between the pair and the rest of the tankmates closely to keep the unpaired siblings safe. In some cases, it is best to leave them in the tank to act as dither fish, attracting the pair's attentions outward in defense mode, and in some cases you will need to remove the unpaired siblings for their own safety.

The best way to get a compatible pair of cichlids like these albino oscars is to raise a group to maturity together in a very large aquarium.

Take It Slow

Unless there is an emergency with your fish, it is best to not act in haste and suddenly pull some out of your tank (even if they're being harassed), but rather to observe and do what is most appropriate for the situation. This is when you will be glad that you have done your research, as each species and each situation is different.

Some species will spawn much more readily in the home aquarium than others. Without even trying, you may one day walk in to find one cichlid hovering over a spot on a log, with another of the same species menacingly holding the rest of the tank inhabitants hostage in a far corner, a female hiding away secretively in a clay pot or a swollen-jawed female concealed in the safe shadows behind a rock.

Remember, a cichlid's sole purpose in life is to ensure that the species will continue to survive into the future. Cichlids *want* to reproduce! If you provide your cichlids with an environment that is close to that of their natural habitat, with consistently clean

water, chances are those cichlids are going to reproduce. If you research your species, find out what their natural environment is like, find out their method of spawning, provide them with water and an aquarium that follows the four keys to success with cichlids that we have discussed, and give them plenty of space, your cichlids will have no reason not to spawn. Granted, there are more difficult species, some that baffle even the most experienced of aquarists, but starting off with the selection of species outlined in Chapter 7 is likely to bring you success!

Conditioning your Cichlids

In the wild, cichlids that are preparing to spawn will store up their food reserves to prepare their bodies for the physical demands that will be placed on them in the weeks ahead. A female that is watching over a clutch of eggs

If you don't notice or realize that some of your cichlids are preparing to mate, finding them guarding a batch of eggs one morning can be quite a surprise.

may not dare to take one moment to feed herself, as a second is all it takes for a predator

to sneak in and gobble up the entire batch. The male, whose job it is to defend the surrounding territory, may have little or nothing to eat as well, since it is his job to keep all intruders from entering the protected zone.

In the case of mouthbrooders, the female will in most cases not feed for up to three weeks once she is holding a mouthful of eggs. Some may snatch a bit of food here or there, but most are relegated to a major fast. In a harem situation, the male not only must have his reserves stored for the many females that he will be courting but also to make sure that no subordinate males are allowed to sneak into the territory and steal his show.

On top of these duties, both the male and female will need the extra reserves they are able to store for the energies expended in the very acts of producing eggs and sperm, and for the ensuing courtship rituals. They will go through several color changes and must prepare the spawning site, all of which uses up the energy they've stored.

To condition your fish in the home aquarium for spawning, begin a feeding regimen that is high in proteins and other nutrients. The perfect fare for conditioning is live foods such as those discussed in Chapter 5. Blackworms, earthworms,

Grindal worms, and white worms are all excellent choices offered in a daily dose to those cichlids whose digestive systems can manage such rich foods. These worms are not to be fed to *Tropheus* or other herbivorous species with long intestines. Live brine shrimp and *Daphnia*, as well as a variety of the frozen foods available, such as bloodworms and krill, are also superb for small to medium-size cichlids. Continue to intermittently feed commercial pellets, flakes, or wafers, and be certain to maintain the vegetable-based food.

Triggering the Spawn

The regular water changes that you are already performing are the perfect inducer for a cichlid spawn. Clean, fresh water is as close to natural as you can get, and when you are changing their water on a regular basis, the chances are great that your cichlids will be triggered to spawn.

Many regions inhabited by cichlids in the wild have a rainy season and a dry season. After a dry spell, the rains pour, the rivers flood, the insects come out and multiply, the food is abundant, the water is fresh, and (you guessed it) the cichlids spawn! Try imitating this at home. Do large water changes each day, dropping the temperature of the water that the tank is replenished with by 5 degrees, just as the rain that falls is cooler than that of the river or lake. Also, if you perform one of these massive water changes just as a storm hits your area and the barometer drops, you have an even better chance of triggering a spawning. A rise in the temperature may also trigger a spawning in some species.

When you are ready to move into trying the more advanced species of cichlids, you will need to think about water chemistry, as some cichlids live in hard water and some in soft water. The pH of the water also varies, with some cichlids living in a pH of 5, or even lower, and some cichlids living in a pH of up to 9. You will then add to your now growing collection some test kits that will give you the readings for the hardness of your water and for the pH. You may then decide to alter the water that comes from your tap, either softening it by running it through peat or hardening it by running it through dolomite, adding dolomite to the substrate, or adding a commercial Rift Lake salt mix made specifically for the purpose. Some species can be maintained adequately without altering the water to suit their natural environment but still require the appropriate hardness and pH in order to reproduce.

Aggression Management

The aggression expressed during courtship and breeding can become quite unruly, particularly within the walls of our aquariums. Never offered a dull moment, playing referee is another challenge that we undertake in our role as keepers of cichlids. You have provided abundant hiding places with rocks, pots, PVC piping, and any other device you can think of, but your male *Vieja synspila* is throttling your female *V. synspila* mercilessly. She is up in the corner of the tank, her fins clamped to her sides, half of her tail ripped off, a hole torn out of her side, and the massive male is gearing up for another charge in his heightened state of unsatisfied sexual arousal, and heading straight for her. At this point you need to grab the net—quickly!

When you decide that it is time for you to encourage your cichlids to breed, it is a good idea to start up at least one more tank. This tank will be used for

Know Your Cichlids

Researching your species is the best way to find out whether one of these methods is likely to trigger a spawning. *Tropical Fish Hobbyist* and other magazines offer numerous articles on breeding specific species, and they often include reports on exciting new breakthroughs in breeding!

emergencies such as this one, or for fry. It is also advisable to go to your local hardware store and purchase a sheet of egg crate, the white plastic grid used to cover fluorescent light fixtures, and have it handy in case of emergencies. If a problem between a male and female does occur, simply place the egg crate vertically into the tank to divide it into two sections, using suction cups from old heaters (of course, saved in your collection of fish stuff) to hold it in position. Make sure Mr. Hot-to-Trot is on one side and the victimized female is on the other. The female should be fed well and given plenty of water changes, secluded shelter, and time to heal behind the safety of her egg crate wall (which obviously must have no holes large enough for the male to squeeze through), leaving the male to fret it out, pacing back and forth on the other side.

As the female heals, cut a hole in the egg crate that is small enough so that only she can get through. When she is back up to speed, one day you are likely to find the female over on the male's side, ready to get on with the business of raising a family. If the male becomes too rambunctious, the female can slip unharmed back through the hole to her own quarters. Actually, some species such as *V. synspila* will spawn right through the egg crate. Place a large clay pot, preferably with the bottom cut out, in with the female.

Turn the pot on its side with the wide opening close to the egg crate. The female will clean and prepare the site inside the pot, just as if the male were with her. The two will court through the egg crate, she will lay her eggs inside the pot, and he will fertilize the eggs through the hole in the wall. Soon you will have fry, and the female will remain safe as she bustles about caring for her young. As the young grow, some will eventually venture through the egg crate, where the male will proudly herd them around in his half of the household.

Hatching the Eggs and Raising the Fry

Once your cichlids have spawned, you will find yourself dealing with a new set of challenges. If all goes as it occurs in nature either one or both parents will take care of the eggs until they hatch. If the species is a substrate spawner, the eggs are guarded with fierce devotion and fanned gently, usually by the female, to keep the oxygenated water circulating around them and any dirt from settling on them. If any eggs turn white with fungus, the female carefully picks those off so that the other eggs are not affected. In a biparental pairing, typically the male keeps a vigilant watch on the outer boundaries of the breeding territory, allowing no intruders near. In about four days the fry will hatch at a temperature of 78° to 80°F (26° to 27°C). The warmer the

Movin' On Up

The parents of many species will dig a pit in another area of the aquarium, pick the newly hatched fry up in their mouths, and carry them to the pit to be deposited in their new nesting site. Do not be surprised to walk in and see no fry where they were when you left them, only to discover that they are elsewhere in the tank! Such moves may actually occur several times over the course of this phase of fry rearing.

water is, the sooner the eggs will hatch. At this point the fry still have a yolk sac attached to them, and they will feed from that for a few more days while the parents continue their jobs of fanning and defending them. Spinning in tiny circles, gathering momentum, and taking short leaps up into the water column only to flutter softly back to the bottom, fry are known as "wrigglers" at this stage.

Once the egg sac is consumed and the fry swim up into the water, they will need to eat. Newly hatched baby brine shrimp is the perfect food for most fry, offering them the optimum nutrients for their young bodies to begin growth into strong adults. The sponge filter of your aquarium and the algae in the tank are excellent food sources too. As the fry begin to mature and turn into young juveniles, the parents continue to watch over and care for them, both performing their assigned duties of hovering about the group, doing their best to keep them clustered in one feeding area, and fending off other tankmates. Eventually, you might find that the young are beginning to disappear. If you want to raise them to adulthood, this is the time to move the young into a separate tank—the parents or other tankmates are more than likely eating them.

Better Safe Than Sorry

In a perfect world, you would always get to enjoy watching eggs grow into fry and eventually beautiful adult cichlids. Unfortunately, we don't live in such a world. You might check your aquarium one day to discover that the eggs, or the

If eggs are disappearing, you can always move some to a plastic container and hatch them yourself.

fry, have totally disappeared. The eggs or the fry can be eaten by the parents or by other predatory tankmates at any stage of the game.

The first time that a pair spawns, try leaving the eggs with the parents. If the eggs disappear, you might decide to let the parents try once or twice more on their own. Sometimes the parents are still young themselves and just need a few trial runs. Sometimes the confines of the aquarium are too great a factor for the parents to overcome. If your cichlids continue to eat their eggs, you can resort to taking the eggs out and hatching them artificially. Try moving the eggs from one batch to another tank, or even a secure plastic container with an aerator, and raising them yourself.

Keep the temperature of the water in this backup container the same as that of your main aquarium's water. An easy way to do this is to float the plastic container on the top of your aquarium water, as long as it's securely attached to the side of the tank so there's no danger of its being tipped over by boisterous tankmates.

Once the fry have hatched and become wrigglers, it is critical that you change the water in the container every day, if not twice a day, at this age. It is easy to do the changes; just be certain to do them very gently, since the fry are fragile and a slight abrasion can cause spinal injury and a deformed adult in the future. Very carefully place the fry and some water from the tank into your trusty dipper or other container, and then

A Helpful Precaution

Mouthbrooding cichlids will hold their eggs for up to three weeks, during which time the female, or in some cases the male, will probably not eat. Some of these species will care for their young, while others will end their parental responsibilities once the young are released from the mouth. Placing the mouthbrooding cichlid into a 5- or 10-gallon (19- or 38-l) tank while it is holding eggs in its buccal cavity is a good way of ensuring that it is not harassed and the fry are not consumed by voracious tankmates once they are released.

> *The world of cichlids has so much beauty, wonder, and fun to offer that no one should miss out on it.*

SMALL FRY

Cichlids and Our Youth

Many of us cichlidophiles started our first cichlid tank in our childhood and from then on never looked back. Cichlids bring the wondrous joys of nature into young people's lives, showing them the beauty to be found in all creatures and bringing with them a sense of responsibility for their care, and education through observing their fascinating behavior. Bring a cichlid or two into a young person's life! You both will be glad that you did!

dispose of the dirty water from the main plastic container that they were in, wipe down the sides, and refill it with fresh water from your cichlid aquarium. Gently place the fry back into their plastic container. They will not even know they have been moved, and will grow in leaps and bounds, ready to graduate into a 5- or 10-gallon (19-or 38-l) tank in no time! The secrets are patience, gentleness, good food, and water changes!

Parting Thoughts

Read and Research

Enough cannot be said for reading and doing your research on cichlids. There are many exceptional books on the subject, and a listing of some excellent suggestions can be found in the next pages of this book. Collecting books on cichlids and related topics is another favorite pastime among cichlidophiles.

Join a Local Club

Most regions have an aquarium club that is within reasonable driving distance, and some aquarists have even been known to drive three hours or more to attend their club's meetings. The monthly meeting draws people together from all walks of life to spend the evening enjoying the camaraderie of one another and to just talk cichlids. Some of the clubs cover all tropical fish, and some are specifically for cichlids. Whichever, you are certain to find abundant hobbyists who share the same passion for cichlids as you do.

Each monthly meeting features a speaker who presents a program on any number of topics, and most clubs have a bowl show in which you can actually enter your own fish. There may be door prizes, raffles, refreshments, a monthly publication, and an auction of fish and plants bred by club members.

Join a National Organization

The American Cichlid Association (ACA) is the largest and most distinguished national organization of the cichlid hobby, founded in 1968 by some of the most respected names in the world of cichlids, many of them still actively involved in research and conservation, and dedicated to spreading their knowledge among hobbyists such as you.

Every July the ACA holds a huge convention, an event that you absolutely will not want to miss! Hundreds of cichlidophiles gather for a long weekend of non-stop world-renowned speakers, a huge cichlid show filled with the most exquisite cichlids beyond your grandest of imaginings, vendors with cichlid supplies, and tanks filled with cichlids for sale. On top of all of that, Sunday features a massive cichlid auction such as you have never witnessed before! I look forward to seeing *you* at the next ACA convention in July!

Enjoy!!!

Now comes the best part of all—have fun, and enjoy spending time with your cichlids!

Resources

Magazines

Tropical Fish Hobbyist
1 T.F.H. Plaza
3rd & Union Avenues
Neptune City, NJ 07753
Phone: (732) 988-8400
E-mail: info@tfh.com
www.tfhmagazine.com

Internet Resources

A World of Fish
www.aworldoffish.com

Aquarium Hobbyist
www.aquariumhobbyist.com

Cichlidfish.com
www.cichlidfish.com

Cichlid Forum
www.cichlid-forum.com

Cichlids of Lake Malawi
www.malawicichlids.com

FINS: The Fish Information Service
http://fins.actwin.com

Fish Geeks
www.fishgeeks.com

Fish Index
www.fishindex.com

Oscarfish.com
www.oscarfish.com

Tropical Resources
www.tropicalresources.net

Associations & Societies

American Cichlid Association
Claudia Dickinson, Membership
Coordinator
P.O. Box 5078
Montauk, NY 11954
Phone: (631) 668-5125
E-mail: IvyRose@optonline.net
www.cichlid.org

Association of Aquarists
David Davis, Membership Secretary
2 Telephone Road
Portsmouth, Hants, England
PO4 0AY
Phone: 01705 798686

Federation of American Aquarium Societies
Jane Benes, Secretary
923 Wadsworth Street
Syracuse, NY 13208-2419
Phone: (513) 894-7289
E-mail: jbenes01@yahoo.com
www.faas.info

American Society of Ichthyologists and Herpetologists
Maureen Donnelly, Secretary
Florida International University
Biological Sciences
11200 SW 8th Street
Miami, FL 33199
Phone: (305) 348-1235
Fax: (305) 348-1986
E-mail: asih@fiu.edu
www.asih.org

Index

109

Index

111

Dedication

To my father, Dwight "Subsee" Smith, who brought me the joy at a very young age of discovering and appreciating the beauties of nature through his eyes.

To you, the hobbyist, in whose hands lies the future of our cichlids.

With deep appreciation to David Boruchowitz, inimitable editor, treasured friend.

And as always, to my dear "Dash."

About the Author

Claudia Dickinson is the author of numerous fishkeeping articles, which have appeared in magazines such as *Tropical Fish Hobbyist*, *Cichlid News*, *Buntbarsche Bulletin*, and *Modern Aquarium*. Claudia has been recognized with significant awards from the Federation of Aquarium Societies, the Northeast Council of Aquarium Societies, the American Cichlid Association, and the Greater City Aquarium Society. She currently is serving her fourth term on the American Cichlid Association's board of trustees, is a life member of the organization, and holds, among others, the position of managing editor of the group's *Buntbarsche Bulletin*. Her roughly 60 home aquaria, totaling 2,500 gallons, focus on cichlids from South America, Central America, Madagascar, and West Africa.

Photo Credits

Mitch Aunger, 26
Andy Lim, 52
Florin Cirstoc, 106
Nikita Rogul, 107
All other photos courtesy of T.F.H. photo archives

REACH OUT. ACT. RESPOND.

Go to AnimalPlanet.com/ROAR and find out how you can be a voice for animals everywhere!

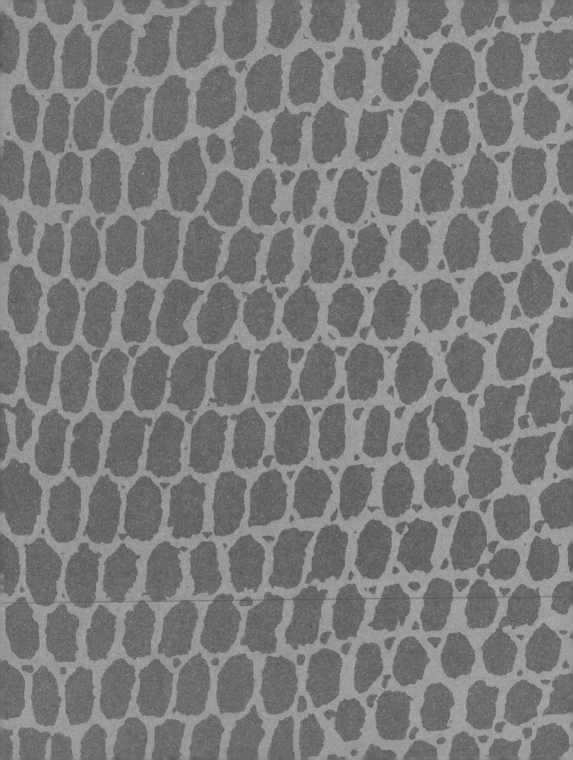